HOW TO BUY A HOME
WITH NO OR POOR CREDIT

HOW TO BUY A HOME WITH NO OR POOR CREDIT

THOMAS K. MASTERS

JOHN WILEY & SONS, INC.
New York • Chichester • Brisbane • Toronto • Singapore

Copyright © 1996 by Thomas K. Masters.
Published by John Wiley & Sons, Inc.

Library of Congress Cataloging-in-Publication Data:

Masters, Thomas K.
    How to buy a home with no or poor credit / by Thomas K. Masters.
      p.   cm.
    Includes bibliographical references (p.   ).
    ISBN 0-471-11996-2 (pbk. : alk. paper)
    1. Mortgage loans—United States.   2. House buying—United States.
   3. Consumer credit—United States.
   HG2040.6.U5M373   1996
   332.7'22'0973—dc20   95-39203

Printed in the United States of America

10 9 8 7 6 5 4 3 2 1

To the late, great,
William P. "Bid" Masters,
my Dad, for all the wisdom and knowledge
passed on through the years.

PREFACE

I began my real estate career in the early 1980s, when the interest rates were between 15 and 16 percent, the economy in the area was depressed, listed properties were abundant, and sales were scarce—a buyer's market, to say the least. I worked in a small real estate office in Palm Springs, California, and in the beginning it was difficult for people to take me seriously in a field where the average age of agents was 35 to 45. Not only did I look young, I was. Through determination, hard work, and staying power, I remained in a tough market; and in 1985 I moved on to an even tougher one, mortgage banking.

I remember my euphoria when I purchased my first home and can still recall my pride as I pressed the garage door opener to pull my car in. I hope that this book will help others experience and enjoy that same pride of home ownership. As a top producer in my field, my goal is to impart a workable knowledge of buying and financing in today's marketplace.

It has been my pleasure to impart the knowledge and expertise I have in obtaining real estate. I hope this publication will serve as a reference guide for you, the reader, now and in the future, in your attempt to obtain real estate and clear your own credit profile.

I sincerely wish you the best.

ACKNOWLEDGMENTS

Special thanks for all your help in preparing my manuscript for publication:

Margo Maley, Waterside Productions, Cardiff By The Sea, California.

Mike Hamilton, John Wiley & Sons, Inc., New York.

Lin Masters, preediting.

Mike Zuckerman, owner, The Mortgage Center, Palm Desert, California.

D&A Credit Reporting Agency, La Quinta, California.

CONTENTS

INTRODUCTION

Every year in the United States, more than three million families buy a home. It is safe to say that at least as many families will start thinking about it. If you are a "would-be" buyer, you probably are aware that purchasing a home is a major undertaking. The process is complicated by issues of financing, as well as by the importance of choosing a home in an area that offers future security and economic wellness.

This book is designed for both first-time buyers and experienced purchasers. Using nontechnical language, it describes techniques for acquiring a home without having to apply for credit, how to buy with no credit, and how to buy with poor credit. *How to Buy a Home with No or Poor Credit* will help you understand the purchase process as well as many alternative mortgage programs. It will serve as a guide and provide you with options you might not have known were available.

I have included chapters on financing a home purchase without the red tape of a conventional loan. The sluggish economy, especially in California, has created some hard times for the average buyer: Many jobs have been lost because of military bases closing, factories sizing down, or companies moving outside the United States. My goal is to increase the overall number of home buyers by highlighting new angles in obtaining a home.

The last thing I want, however, is to motivate my readers to purchase a home they cannot afford. I will explain the guidelines for "qualifying ratios" set by the federal lending authorities, as well as explain the individual roles of the Federal Housing Administration (FHA), Veterans Administration (VA), the Federal National Mortgage Association (FNMA, or "Fannie Mae"), and the Federal Home Loan Mortgage Corporation (FHLMC, or "Freddie Mac"). By following the guidelines, you won't tend to overextend yourself as you enter the real estate buying process. You don't want or need a *foreclosure* on your record. If you read carefully, not only will you learn the techniques of home buying, you will learn about affording the payment, while enjoying the equity appreciation and tax advantages.

If you have "no" or "poor" credit because of past job losses, divorce, or death of a wage earner, you too may achieve home ownership again: This book can be used by anyone regardless of credit rating. I also will assume that the reader has no knowledge about buying a home such as loan qualification guidelines, the types of loans available, and the pitfalls and potential problems.

I will explain in simple terminology how to take the first step in purchasing a home. When you *do* take that step, you will be confident that you know the value of your property, have the ability to repay, and can make an offer that will satisfy the selling party or lending institution. If you apply yourself and are willing to take a chance, you will be surprised how easy buying a home can be.

This book is *not* written to be a "no money down," "get rich quick," or "make a million in real estate" advice manual; its purpose is to help you learn the basics of home buying so that you can turn your dream of ownership into reality. You will think about the different ways to construct a purchase between buyer and seller that will benefit you most. The text covers the following subjects:

In Chapter 1, I will explain the FHA nonqualifying loan and ways to obtain this financing without qualifying for a home loan; also the FHA streamline refinance procedure.

In Chapter 2, I will explain the VA loan—assumptions without qualifying.

Chapter 3 describes seller carryback financing and wrap around mortgages (no new loan involved).

Chapter 4 deals with lease with option for instant equity.

In Chapter 5, I will explain equity sharing and how to buy without applying for a loan.

Chapter 6 describes how to obtain income through home equity.

Chapter 7 covers the process of obtaining homes at a discount through bank-owned properties and HUD-insured properties.

In Chapter 8, you will learn about hard money loans and quick qualifier loans.

In Chapter 9, I will explain how to obtain deferredly maintained or damaged properties and how to finance all the repairs into your purchase.

Chapter 10 is devoted to the role of the mortgage banker: what to look for in choosing a lender.

In Chapter 11, you will find out how to qualify for low down and no down payment home loans. It includes the guidelines in prequalifying for a home loan, the basics, the ratios, and the necessary requirements.

Chapter 12 provides step-by-step instructions for completing the application, the questions, and the forms for a home loan.

In Chapter 13, I will show you what to look for in interest rates, how to find the best loan programs available, and how to get approval for such a loan.

Chapter 14 explores the methods for cleaning up your credit by telephone.

Chapter 15 describes how to clean up your credit in writing, including form letters and procedures in keeping with the Fair Credit Reporting Act.

1 FEDERAL HOUSING ADMINISTRATION ASSUMPTION: NONQUALIFYING LOANS

ANY FHA LOAN ORIGINATED PRIOR TO DECEMBER 31, 1986 REQUIRES NO QUALIFYING!

Yes, this is true. You too can find this type of creative financing. The Federal Housing Administration (FHA) is the insuring body for the Department of Housing and Urban Development. Created in the 1930s, the FHA loan program was designed to assist the average American in buying real estate with a very low down payment. With approximately 3 percent down, home buyers can obtain financing through banks and savings and loans (and now mortgage companies) whose mortgages are insured by the Federal Housing Administration (FHA). In this way, the lender's risk is minimal; if a buyer defaults, the lender can regain all losses through the mortgage insurance.

An assumable loan is a loan that can be taken over by the buyer of a property. The buyer continues to make the payments as structured originally by the lender; the term of the loan (usually 30 years) does not change, nor does the interest rate. If the seller has made mortgage payments for 8 years of the 30-year term, the buyer assumes the loan with the remaining 22 years left on the loan. The advantage to the buyer is that the lower the loan term (in years) the more the mortgage payments reduce the principal each month.

The term *qualifying* refers to the process of determining a buyer's eligibility for credit and/or ability to repay a credit obligation. When searching for a nonqualifying loan (a loan that a buyer may assume without having to support income, employment, or creditworthiness), ask your real estate agent to look for sellers with existing FHA financing on their property. Sometimes, a seller who is motivated to sell may allow the buyer to assume the existing loan without qualifying (as long as the loan was originated prior to December 31, 1986). The seller might be motivated to sell for a number of reasons: job transfer, divorce, death in the family, or reduced income. Such sellers are often willing to work out a deal with a sincere buyer.

Although you might assume this loan, the seller's credit will still show the loan in his or her name and the seller will be held responsible for up to five years for any and all late payments. If you go into a default position, the previous owner is usually the first person contacted, and it's possible that the original owner may take the house back prior to a full foreclosure proceeding. Because of the declining values (and corresponding loss of equity) of properties since early 1993, these FHA loans may be more readily available now than in past years.

When searching for an FHA-assumable loan, have your realtor scan for current listings, which should be easily accessed through their computerized multiple listing service. When you find a suitable property, find out how long the owner has been in the home and whether he or she assumed an FHA loan that was originated prior to December 1986 (these loans can be assumed time and time again). A new buyer or owner has to have owned the property for at least 12 months. These real estate loans do not require that the property be your primary residence, as do the brand-new FHA loans that people qualify for today.

After December 1, 1986, the assumption rules changed for FHA-insured properties. Credit checks became required, yet were not always completed. A buyer may assume an existing FHA loan, *subject to,* which means the seller is solely responsible in the event of a default. There is one way to obtain an FHA loan without qualifying for it if you assume an existing FHA loan originated after 1986. I have helped borrowers do this dozens of times. What they do is purchase the property, having the title changed into their name. If they make 12 months' payments on time, and can provide canceled checks to substantiate same, they are eligible for an FHA streamline refinance, which requires no credit check and no income verification (see FHA streamline later in this chapter). As long as the note rate is higher than the current interest rate, the lender will approve the loan with just a loan application; therefore no appraisal or credit check would be required (other than 12 months' canceled checks for house payments) and a request for *payoff or demand,* as it is properly called. If you purchase a property requiring qualification for an assumable loan, the fees involved are $250 application and $250 assumption fee (a great savings that surely beats paying closing costs and impound fees, usually 3% of the sales price).

I received a phone call one afternoon from a contractor in the Palm Springs area. I had never done any business with him, but he inquired about refinancing his own home (owner/builder) in Sky Valley, California—an underdeveloped area just 15 miles from Palm Springs. This custom home was situated in an area where homes were on 2½- to 5-acre parcels.

Just down the street from his home was a two-bedroom, two-bath home, of approximately 1,200 square feet, with a two-car garage. Large tamarisk trees bordered the block wall that surrounded it. And there was a reason for such privacy! The previous owner had been using the property to cultivate illegal substances for the purpose of sales. The property was left vacant when the San Bernardino Sheriff's Department came in, arrested the owner (whose operations were detected with aerial photos), and sent him off to jail.

The contractor contacted the lender of the property, verified it was in default, and learned that the loan on the property was fully assumable with no qualifying.

There was an existing FHA loan on the property at 10.5 percent interest (fixed rate). The contractor prepared an offer and negotiated with the previous owner (now in prison) through his attorney. With just $2,000 down, he was able to take over the existing loan and the property by executing a *quitclaim deed* (a legal document used to remove or add an individual or individuals to title to show ownership interest), thereby taking the previous owner off title. The balance on the loan was just $41,000 and the property today is worth $85,000. Although 10.5 percent interest sounds high, the rates were much higher in the early 1980s. Although the contractor obtained this property through the misfortune of another, it's a reminder that you should *keep your eyes open*.

THE FHA STREAMLINE REFINANCE

To explain how a buyer can obtain financing without qualifying for a home loan, I will begin by sharing a transaction that I closed early in 1994.

A married couple came to me through a referral from a previous client. They had purchased a home from a seller who needed to get out of his payment because the seller's wife had lost her job and they were having trouble making ends meet. My clients took over the existing FHA loan, which had a payoff of approximately $122,000 at a fixed interest rate of 10.5 percent. The current market at the time was in the 8.5 percent range. The buyers agreed to refinance the property within the first two years to relieve the seller of his liability. Since the interest rate was lower than the note rate, the buyers became eligible for the FHA streamline refinance.

I met with my clients, filled out the 1003 (application), and began explaining the program to them. Much to their surprise, they did not have to qualify for a home loan. The FHA streamline requires a few basic things: a loan application and a mortgage rating (only) or copies of 12 months' canceled checks (front and back) to prove payments were made. When my clients bought this property, they took over an existing FHA loan that left the seller responsible for the debt. Now the thinking behind this type of refinance is that, if the borrower can pass the test of making 12 months' payments on time, and the payments under the refinance are going to go down, then he or she obviously can make the lower payment.

During the refinance boom of the late 1980s and early 1990s, this was a popular program for people who had obtained real estate by taking over an existing FHA loan. In retrospect, they obtained home ownership without ever qualifying for a loan, and never had to have a credit report pulled.

Streamline financing is only for those people converting from an existing FHA loan to either a lower loan term, such as a 30-year to a 15-year (you must save at least $50 per month to change your term) or from a fixed-rate to an FHA adjustable-rate to accomplish the same.

The FHA adjustable-rate mortgage is one of the best programs available for financing, as it is usually tied to the Treasury bill or 1-year T-bill. The advantage of this is that the T-bill is a slow moving index tied to what the banks are paying for their money. The adjustable rate cannot go up more than 1 percent annually, so depending on the change date, individuals starting in the 6 percent range could be at just 9 percent at the end of 36 to 42 months. Since the majority of homeowners only stay in their homes on an average of three to five years, a buyer can take advantage of the savings between the fixed rate that they could have had and the adjustable rate they accepted, which is lower. As the homeowner's needs change (e.g., family growth, employment changes, promotions, economic changes), a borrower might become eligible to move on to a bigger and better property. By this time, the home buyer will have realized some equity to use for the purchase of the next home.

The FHA streamline adjustable loan has no negative amortization and has almost replaced the *FHA 245 GPM* (graduated payment mortgage), a popular program in the early 1980s. If you are thinking about assuming an FHA 245 GPM, *think again!* These loans have a negative amortization, meaning the original loan balance, or principal, *increases;* the note rate is not enough to cover the interest due on the loan. *The unpaid interest is added to the principal, and you will end up owing more money than you borrowed.* This program was originally set up with the understanding that because interest rates were so high in the 1980s, FHA home buyers could qualify for a home loan at a low start rate, increasing annually up to 7.5 percent of the payment each year.

I had a client involved in the FHA 245 GPM program whose original deed of trust had been $67,000. She was interested in refinancing to a fixed rate to get out of the negative adjustable-rate program. When she received the payoff statement from her mortgage company, she discovered that she owed more than $9,000 in additional principal, after having made payments on the house for five years. Because she loved her home and did not want to lose it, she agreed to the current low fixed rate and her refinance was streamlined.

Again, be careful to check out any existing FHA loan before you assume it. Make sure you know what type of FHA loan it is, what the current rate is and whether it is fixed, adjustable, or a negative GPM from the past.

Many FHA loans are assumed and taken over by borrowers with secondary financing: a second trust deed behind the first. Examples of a second trust deed might be a seller carryback, a swimming pool loan, or a home improvement loan. Regardless of the type of second trust deed, once you are holding title and you want to streamline the first trust deed, you are eligible to do so. The holder of the second trust deed will be sent a subordination agreement by the escrow company or an attorney handling the refinance.

The first trust deed (an instrument that transfers the bare legal title of a property to a trustee, to be held pending fulfillment of an obligation) is reduced to current market interest rates due to the streamline refinance and the second trust deed is re-recorded by the county in which the property exists. Now you have lowered your payments and kept your second trust deed the same. No credit report was required, and you are now in a home that you have never qualified for.

When you are trying to assume a nonqualifying loan, keep in mind that the maximum FHA loan amounts have changed over the years. In 1986 when loans could be assumed with no qualifying, the maximum loan amount was $90,000. In 1991, the maximum changed to $124,875, and now the maximum loan amount is up to $151,575. These figures can vary from county to county, but for the most part are close to the amounts I have quoted.

When looking for the FHA-assumable loan, ask your real estate broker or agent for a computer printout of such properties. Always consult a licensed agent, broker, or attorney before entering any purchase contract and check my prequalifying guidelines (see Chapter 4) to make sure you can afford your future house payment.

2 VETERANS ADMINISTRATION ASSUMPTIONS

The Veterans Administration, or VA (a federal agency that guarantees loans), has "nonqualifying" assumable loans that veterans of the armed forces had qualified for at one time, and are available to *you* whether or not you are a veteran. These nonqualifying loans *must have been originated prior to March 1, 1988*.

The VA guarantees a loan up to $203,000 (1996 figures), no money down, which guarantees the lender a return of up to 25 percent of the loan in the event of default (nonpayment). The original buyer would send in a copy of their DD214 (Discharge Form) along with a VA 1880 Form which is a Request for Eligibility. When the certificate of eligibility is returned; it will have a dollar figure indicting full entitlement for the loan, which would be 25 percent of the maximum VA loan amount. The figure indicated on the certificate is what VA will guarantee the lender against the borrower's default.

The original borrower had to qualify as to income, job stability, cash reserves, and credit. The VA has since then raised their "no money down" loan limits, and loans after March 1, 1988, require qualifying.

A seller who allows you to assume an existing loan will still be responsible for the payments if you go into default. The FHA limits the responsibility of the seller or original borrower to five years, whereas the VA does not. If the veteran (seller) insists on obtaining a release of liability form, you, the buyer, will have to qualify for the assumption with some form of credit.

Do not get discouraged, as literally millions of VA or GI Bill loans have been originated and you will still find sellers who have fallen on hard times and need to get out from under their house payments. When assuming a VA loan, always consider the loan term—how many years are remaining and the interest rate in which it was originally written.

Here are some points to consider: You do not have to be a veteran to assume a VA loan, nor does the property you are buying have to be your primary residence, as it would if you were buying it as a veteran using your VA eligibility. This means you could assume an existing VA loan that was originated prior to March 1, 1988, and use the property as an investment or second home or live in it as your primary residence. The VA has payment collection policies that would affect the veteran who qualified for the loan, so the VA seller might need some convincing as to your ability to repay. If the veteran allows you to assume an existing loan, he or she may be giving up the entitlement to purchase with "no down" or lose a portion of the equity.

Most buyers assuming existing VA loans have a clause in their trust deed, being carried by the seller as a junior lien, that indicates the first and second liens will be refinanced within three years of recording. This gives the borrower time to establish credit and possibly obtain increases in pay. A spouse could be working on a degree and be employed by then. Other factors may finally release a seller from liability, or make the person eligible again for "no down VA financing." The new homeowners can either buy-up (purchase a larger property with a higher sales price) or have enough equity in the house to be able to refinance with no cash out-of-pocket.

Be aware that state regulations can sometimes affect financing. Much of my business is in the state of California, so I will use the differences between a VA loan and a Cal-Vet loan as an example:

1. A Cal-Vet loan can be assumed only by another California veteran. A VA loan can be assumed by anyone.

2. A Cal-Vet loan requires a 5 percent down payment, whereas a VA loan requires 0 percent down.

3. A Cal-Vet loan is an adjustable-rate loan, whereas VA loans are fixed *and* adjustable. In the current market, it would be possible to assume a VA loan that originated prior to March 1, 1988, because sales prices are currently plummeting back to those price ranges not only in California, but in many other parts of the United States.

Remember, check any prequalifying guidelines to make sure you can afford your new payment.

3 OWNER OR SELLER FINANCING

When searching for a home and assumable financing is not available on a property in an area you wish to live, one of your best options is to look for a home where the seller will carry the paper. This type of finance would have on the listing agreement or in the newspaper "OWC," or "owner will carry." This form of financing enables the seller to make the property more marketable, especially in a declining economy.

You might ask, why would sellers want to act as a bank and carry the paper on a home they're selling? Well, motivation of some kind is always the weighing factor on negotiated real estate transactions. A seller might agree to carry back the note on a home to realize a better return than would be possible on a bank deposit, certificate, or Treasury bill.

For example, if you find a home with an asking price of $100,000 and a seller who needs to get out from it and is willing to carry the paper, you can obtain title and interest in the house and the seller will receive the payments each month, which become income for the seller and a tax advantage for you, the homeowner.

On a sales price of $100,000, a seller might accept a 10 percent down payment and finance the balance of $90,000. By acting as the bank, the seller would be collecting $750 per month at a 10 percent fixed rate "interest only." In this situation, the seller would record a first deed of trust in his favor with the county recorder in the county the property is in. The interest rate charged by the seller can be negotiated by the buyer and seller, depending on the terms of the purchase, but it usually will be in the same neighborhood as the current fixed rates by banks and savings and loan institutions. This type of recorded deed of trust will be an "interest only," with a clause for a *balloon* payment. A balloon payment, or "balloon note" calls for periodic payments that would not be sufficient to fully amortize the face amount of the note prior to maturity; if "interest only" as in this case, the principal sum known as the "balloon" is due at maturity, or the date agreed on in the note. The reason for the balloon clause in the note is so that the seller can realize the proceeds in 3 to 5 years, without amortizing the loan over a 30-year period. Most "interest only" notes call for a 3- to 5-year term, but you can negotiate a 10-year or 15-year loan, if the seller decides to do so.

The buyer of this property can sell it anytime or refinance it prior to the note term. This will not create a problem unless the seller has a "prepayment penalty" clause in the note, which usually does not happen. A prepayment on a loan usually calls for six months' worth of interest payments as the penalty, but it can vary.

Who would be most likely to carry a large note on a home for a prospective buyer? To name a few, older people planning to retire, or an elderly seller who has become widowed and cannot handle the maintenance and upkeep of a large home. These are good candidates for seller financing, which can provide a stable monthly income and can be willed in the event of death to children or other heirs.

Property in bad condition is a prime candidate for seller financing. Banks and lending institutions have set regulations as to the condition of the property that they will lend on, and if the property is in poor condition, they will not lend against it as security for repayment of the debt. If you are looking for a fixer-upper, a property that needs a lot of cosmetic work or even major work, this kind of property is also good for seller financing and perhaps the only avenue for you to take title and interest in the home.

The seller also may finance for a zoning change. I have seen many older homes that end up on a main street with the zoning changed from residential to commercial. A bank cannot lend on this because if the property had a fire, it could not be replaced as a single family home due to the zoning change, which makes it uninsurable.

I learned this the hard way when I was doing a home loan for a couple in Blythe, California. The borrowers were approved and we were ready to close the escrow, but the property, although single family, was in an area where the zoning had changed to commercial. We could not obtain insurance for this now commercial property, so the mortgage company would not lend on it. Seller financing became our only move to save the deal. The buyers agreed and escrow was eventually closed. When considering seller financing, always make sure that the property you are buying will be marketable when it comes time for you to sell. Also keep in mind that the zoning change can work the opposite way in some cases.

I have a relative who acquired five properties in the mid to late 1980s—Victorian homes in the older portion of Sacramento, California. When the zoning changed from residential to commercial in these areas, the values of the properties increased, so sometimes the zoning variance can be in your favor.

OWNER WRAP TO REFINANCE

A few years back, a client was referred to me after he had met with several lenders in an attempt to refinance his property. *The problem:* He had purchased a home from an individual who carried the paper. In this case, the seller pays off the first trust deed to the bank and the buyer pays the seller direct. This is known as a "wraparound mortgage." It's legal, but risky. The seller carried back a second trust deed; therefore my client, the buyer, was paying the seller directly on the first and second mortgages.

There was a reason my client had difficulty refinancing this property when it came time to do so. Technically, he did not own it! Without the grant deed being recorded in the county in which he resides, the title was "clouded." He was strongly counting on my help to save all the money he had put into the property in the past for improvements and payments inclusive.

By Freddie Mac (Federal Home Loan Mortgage Corporation) guidelines, the buyer needed to show a few basic proofs of ownership. Number 1, he had a grant deed, notarized but not recorded. Number 2, he had been taking the mortgage interest write-off on his tax returns and was able to prove he was making house payments by showing canceled checks. And Number 3, he had to prove that he was making payments on property taxes and hazard insurance.

My client not only provided all the requested documentation, but because we were handling this as a refinance, the second trust deed against the property was his down payment.

The property was appraised at $165,000 and with the balance on the first and second mortgages, plus all closing costs, there was a total due of $115,000. We requested that the grant deed be recorded prior to our company funding the new loan, and before my client knew it, he had a new 30-year loan with a lower interest rate than he had been paying previously, and the only out-of-pocket expenses incurred were for the appraisal and credit report.

Owner wraps are a common way to be creative in financing if a buyer has difficulty qualifying for a loan. Income can change over the term, and eventually you can refinance to pay off the private note or the seller carrying the paper, much like this client did, even after not properly executing a recording on the grant deed.

A few years back, I had a young couple come into my office to see about qualifying for a home loan. Their income was good; they were both working. But they had *one problem:* Due to medical problems of the wife and a lack of medical insurance at the time of these problems, this couple had been forced to file a bankruptcy. By lending standards, a bankruptcy has to be over two years old for the borrower to become eligible for financing a home. They did not know what to do. I had a client for whom I had financed properties in the past, and I remembered he was trying to sell one of his own properties because the tenants had vacated the premises and he was having trouble keeping up with the payments.

I put my client and the couple together and they were able to purchase the house with a "wraparound mortgage" also known as an all-inclusive deed of trust. The wraparound mortgage, or a second or junior mortgage, is defined by the face value of the amount it secures plus the balance due under the first mortgage. The buyer, who now holds title to the property, makes a single payment each month to the seller. In this example, the seller is collecting on a sales price of $150,000 with 10 percent down, thus creating a note of $135,000 at 9 percent interest. The seller's first trust deed payment is still made by himself, at 8 percent fixed, so he is making an additional 1 percent on the first plus 9 percent on the second or junior lien of $25,000 since the seller's payoff figure was only $110,000.

The couple had agreed to refinance within the first 36 months to pay off the first and second trust deeds. The seller was willing to carry the mortgages because of this time limitation followed by the balloon payment (a part of the purchase contract).

The buyers agreed to obtain a new avenue of finance and cash out the seller for whatever the amount is still owed. With this in mind, at the time of purchase, the buyers hope that they will be eligible for new financing at a later date, provided they can meet the qualifying criteria set by either FHA, VA, or conventional financing (FNMA or FHLMC). By that time, more than two years will have elapsed after the bankruptcy, and the young couple will be more established in the workplace and credit world.

When considering a wraparound mortgage, try to negotiate the interest rate as close to current market rates as possible. A reasonable rate would be anything slightly higher than what a seller could get from a money market, CD, T-bill, or bank. And again, refer to my prequalification guidelines (see Chapter 11) to make sure you can afford your house payment.

It's not true that only the rich, educated, and lucky can buy real estate; anyone can own a home if they have the necessary tools and the desire to do so. It is neither difficult nor time-consuming. Once you realize the availability of property and the reasons for its availability, it will make perfect sense to you.

Motivation is always a key when it comes to picking up a property. No-money down deals are few and far between, but you can obtain real estate without having to qualify for a loan if you seek out creative financing. This may involve dealing directly with the lender, clearing your credit to qualify for a loan, assuming an FHA loan, or purchasing a property on an owner wraparound.

Seller financing should not be a complicated transaction, but if there are no real estate agents or brokers to assist you in constructing your offer, make sure you use a reputable escrow company or an attorney (for areas where escrows are not used) to verify that you have obtained legal and clear title before you move in.

4 LEASE WITH OPTION FOR INSTANT EQUITY

The "Lease with Option to Purchase" is not a new program; it's existed for many years. It is seldom suggested by real estate agents and brokers because of the structure of the transaction; they do not receive a commission until the buyer (tenant) in the transaction exercises the option to purchase the house and closes escrow. This could be as long as a year or more.

The seller in this transaction is your landlord. The lease with option to purchase is a good way for the tenant or potential buyer to get a foot into the homeownership door.

The lease with option to purchase starts with a contract between tenant (potential buyer) and landlord (seller). The buyer and seller agree on a specific purchase price that would freeze the price for the future exercise of the option. The buyer and seller further agree on a monthly rental amount with a portion of that rent (sometimes all of it, depending on the contract) to be applied to the purchase price of the house, in the form of a credit toward the down payment or closing costs.

In a *down market,* better known as a "buyer's market," the lease with option to purchase is an attractive avenue to consider if the seller has had the property on the market for a long time.

By freezing the purchase price, the buyer can take advantage of the possible increase in the property's value over the lease term, which is usually one year but sometimes is two years or more. Although the value of the home increases during the lease period, the seller is obligated to sell the house at the previously agreed-on price provided you want to exercise the option to purchase. This can mean instant equity. If the value of the house decreases during the lease term, you are not obligated to exercise your option.

In a no-credit or poor credit situation, the option gives the buyer time either to establish new credit or to clean up the credit problems incurred in the past (see Chapters 14 and 15).

When writing a lease with option to purchase agreement or contract (forms found at local stationery stores or through local real estate broker), the seller (landlord) usually requires a fee called an "option fee" or "option monies." This is a negotiable figure, generally 2 to 3 percent of the negotiated purchase price. For example, a $90,000 sales price might require $2,000 to $3,000 in option monies. *An option fee can be lost if the option is not exercised,* so be careful when signing a lease with option to purchase. Make sure you are happy with the home, the neighborhood, proximity to work, schools, shopping facilities, or whatever amenities your family might need in the near future.

The option fee serves as a partial or full down payment on the home when it comes time to exercise your option, depending on the terms you negotiate with the seller.

Example. A married couple were renting a home when the seller decided to place the subject property on the market. The seller allowed the tenants to apply their first and last months' deposit, totaling $1,500, as option monies. The couple loved the home and by moving into a lease with option to purchase arrangement they avoided having to look for another home, as well as the costly deposits necessary to move in. The seller and buyer agreed on a purchase price of $85,000 and wrote the contract for a one-year period with "rental credit."

Rental payments can be applied toward your down payment and closing costs. Amounts applied toward the purchase price can be as high as 100 percent or as low as 10 percent, depending on your contract and the type of loan you obtain at the end of your lease term.

Assuming an existing loan involves many variables. In Chapters 1 and 2, I explained taking up FHA or VA loans, either when they are fully assumable or are subject to the previous owner's being responsible until the property is sold, refinanced, or five years have passed.

Example—Option Fee and Rental Credit. A buyer and seller agree on a purchase price of $100,000 and enter into a lease with option to purchase transaction. The option fee money up front (or down payment) is 3 percent, totaling $3,000. The seller agrees to give the buyer (tenant) a $1,000 per month rental credit toward the purchase. The term of the lease is one year. The buyer will assume an existing FHA loan against the property, the balance of which is $85,000.

With the sales price at $100,000 and a $3,000 option fee and $12,000 in rental credit at the end of 12 months, the buyer *assumes the existing loan;* the seller has received his equity in the form of down payment or option money, and 12 months' rent. The buyer in this case has purchased a home, and has instant equity of $15,000 in the first year. In this example, the seller was obviously motivated by such a huge rental credit (100%) and allowing a year to go by to repay the debt. Not all leases with options to purchase go that smoothly. But there are some out there like that, so be on the look out.

Another variable in the same scenario would be if the seller only allotted 50 percent of the $1,000 in rental credit. The difference between the first trust deed of $85,000, with $3,000 in option monies and $500 in rental credit would leave a $6,000 balance owing at the end of the lease. Provided the buyer is paying rent on time, the seller may be willing to carry back a second trust deed for $6,000 as a junior lien recorded in the county where the property is located. In such cases, the seller will carry back the second as an "interest only" note, payable in three to five years. In this example, the buyer is still realizing instant equity of $9,000 after the first 12 months.

Both of the preceding examples involved a one-year term on the lease. If a one-year lease term is all a seller is willing to negotiate, make sure you have a renewal option for an extension to stay in the property. The seller may have the right to renegotiate the terms of the lease with option to purchase after the option has expired.

When you have a lease with option to purchase, you will need to choose a method of financing when the time comes to exercise your option. Not all sellers will be gracious enough to carry back paper, nor are all loans assumable. As stated earlier in this chapter, one of the benefits of the lease with option to purchase is that it allows you the time to establish new credit or restore your creditworthiness while securing a piece of real estate for the future.

If you decide to apply for government-insured financing (FHA or VA), the rental credit is determined by the lender under the HUD Manual 4155 underwriting guidelines. For example, if you were paying $1,000 per month rent, of which the seller assigned $500 per month in rental credit, and under your terms of the lease you were to obtain new financing, FHA guidelines could alter that rental credit. When you submit a loan application, your lender will require an appraisal on the property, including a rental survey for a lease option purchase. This means the appraiser has to survey the area for "normal" rents. If the normal rent for a house comparable to yours is $700 per month, then the FHA guidelines will only allow you, as buyer, a $300 rental credit. Although the seller had allowed a $500 rental credit, this $200 differential will be thrown out the window with a government-insured loan; the buyer has no recourse. A capable and competent mortgage banker should know these rules *inside and out* and should be able to guide you in selecting the proper loan option. The HUD Underwriting Manual 4155 explains rental credits; your mortgage broker or banker should have ready access to this information as well.

When entering any purchase transaction, always consult a licensed real estate agent or broker, or an attorney.

5 EQUITY SHARING: BUYING WITHOUT APPLYING FOR A LOAN

Equity sharing is a relatively new concept in acquiring real estate that has increased in popularity since the early 1980s. The concept usually works with close friends or relatives, one of whom makes the payment on a property as well as lives in it, while the other one, the investor or purchaser, qualifies for the loan.

An investor might look for a property that has been deferredly maintained and needs primarily cosmetic attention (e.g., paint, carpeting, landscaping). By taking on an equity partner, the person living in the house would make the payment and go on the title with the owner, as a *tenant in common* with a 50 percent ownership. This makes the two people on title, partners or equity partners. In a "best case" scenario, the properties in the area increase in value and because the buyer purchased the house in relatively poor condition, the owners could quickly realize an equity or profit position by making the improvements. In addition, both parties will realize a tax break (consult your tax authority on deductions). The usual contract time frame between equity partners is three to five years. Most properties, if purchased during correct market situations, will increase in value over this time frame.

COHABITING EQUITY PARTNERS

Another type of equity sharing occurs when the investor lives in the property with the partner. I financed a home for a client who qualified for a loan and brought his friend on title as an equity partner, although the friend or partner would not have been able to qualify for a loan. After 12 months, the investor accepted a job transfer out of the area and no longer wanted to remain responsible for the loan, which was in his name. Because the partner had showed good faith in continuing the mortgage payments, the investor allowed the partner to take full Title of the property and settled for an equity split, or the amount the investor had into the property up until that time.

Equity sharing is not limited to the single-family residences. The Department of Housing and Urban Development provides a HUD Repo List every week, for all counties. Investors can buy two to four units with just 15 percent down, which is an attractive loan for an investor. Lawyers, doctors, and others in high-income brackets are always looking for a good tax writeoff. In a sense, taking an equity partner means the investor acquires a built-in apartment manager, maintenanceperson, and groundskeeper, to handle the investment.

OWNER OCCUPIED EQUITY SHARING

If you own no other property (via FHA), you can purchase a two- to four-unit property and live in one of the units with a 3.5 to 5 percent down payment, add on your equity partner, and realize rents to help cover the rest of your payments. This is an excellent way to get started if you find the investor who will bring you in as a partner.

EQUITY SHARING VACATION HOME

You also can use equity sharing within your own family. I know of a family who purchased a property in Lake Arrowhead,

California, a seasonal resort community offering skiiing in the winter and boating during the summer. The family pooled their monies to qualify for the loan, and when escrow closed, the additional partners were named on title. This type of equity sharing is a good investment because a rental agent manages the property, and keeps it rented when the principal partners are not enjoying it. As time goes on, the equity will increase, and the entire family will enjoy a piece of the pie when they sell the property, not to mention having a good writeoff in the meantime.

EQUITY SHARING WITH SELLER

Another form of equity sharing is taking over a loan from a seller who has fallen on hard times and is close to losing a property. In return for curing the late payments, the seller would award you half interest in the house and allow you to come on title as half owner or partner. You would not have to qualify for a home loan as the financing is already in place on the house.

For example, a real estate broker had tenants in a property who left it in very poor condition. The broker so frustrated at having to replace the carpet, paint the interior, and fix the landscaping just to make it rentable again, was ready to give up his loan on the property (15 year, 8.5% fixed) with only 12 years remaining on the loan. I had a close friend who was making good money at the time, but he had been through a divorce and his credit was not in good standing. Knowing he was interested in getting back on his feet, I put the two parties together. They struck an equity-sharing deal in which the broker allowed my friend to move in, and make the necessary payments and repairs for a 50 percent interest. Because the loan had only 12 more years on it, every time a payment was made, the equity increased much more rapidly than it would have if it had been a 30-year loan. Both parties were satisfied, and the broker was spared the nightmarish risk of renting the property to destructive tenants again.

UPS AND DOWNS OF EQUITY SHARING

Now that I have listed some examples of equity sharing, let me explain the ins and outs of equity sharing. Equity sharing can be an intense purchase process and should definitely involve a real estate agent or real estate broker, or even an attorney. I suggest this to the first-time buyer. If you have participated in equity sharing in the past, you already know the potential monies to be made, and the risks involved.

Equity sharing carries the same risks as other types of home buying, but you are involving yourself with a family member, a friend, or even a total stranger. During the equity-sharing period, property depreciation, neighborhood changes, the death of a wage earner, and job loss are among the possibilities that can affect the arrangement.

A real estate agent can help you understand transactions of this type so you don't go in blindfolded. He or she should explain the types of loans that are available, how to prequalify for financing, and the kind of property that might best suit your needs. The agent can use the multiple listing service to locate offerings that will match your requirements for schools, square footage of the home, price range, and so forth. Your agent also will know the type of financing the seller is looking for. Desperate sellers sometimes will give a share of the equity to a buyer who can come in with enough cash to make up back payments, and pay the commission and closing costs.

As a buyer, it is definitely to your advantage to use the services of a real estate agent because it costs you nothing to do so. Real estate sales commissions are *paid by the seller* by virtue of a signed listing agreement.

Your agent may never even meet the seller personally, but only the seller's agent, since in most real estate transactions, the seller's agent presents the buyer's offer to the seller. Occasionally, the buyer's agent requests to present the offer, and in this case, usually both agents will show up at the "offer presentation." When your real estate agent is representing both buyer and seller, this must be disclosed, and the agent has a fiduciary obligation to work diligently in both favors. Some agents do sell their own listings.

When you decide to make an offer, always keep in mind that the asking price is not automatically the sales price. That's why they call an offer, an "offer." You are making a "bid" on the house and usually start lower than the sales price, or listed price. Your real estate agent will guide you by showing you sales prices over the course of the past six-month period for properties with similar features and comparable square footages.

When the offer has been written and all contingencies of the offer have been met (e.g., financing, inspections, appraisal, clear title), monies for closing are deposited into escrow for that purpose.

Escrow agents act as a neutral, third party between buyer and seller. Most states use either escrow agents or the escrow department of a title insurance company. In states that do not use escrow, an attorney would act as a closing agent. During an escrow period, the escrow agent would send out escrow instructions for both the buyer and seller reflecting the terms of the purchase agreement. Escrow would also order a preliminary title report or search, which would give both parties an idea of the liens currently being held against the property. This report would also specify any utility easements.

Escrow is responsible for the disbursement of all funds, at closing. These funds include the down payment made into escrow, the payoff, and reconveyance of the old mortgage, the monies disbursed to the seller for the net proceeds, and all commissions and other fees to be paid. The new loan or loans are recorded prior to monies being disbursed. Escrow then sends a settlement statement or HUD 1 to all parties in the transaction so they know where and how all monies have been disbursed. Any overages are refunded directly to the buyer (most escrow companies collect a pad of approximately $200 so they don't come up short).

When an equity share transaction is formulated properly, things usually go smoothly because there has been a meeting of the minds between the parties involved. To make a smooth equity share transaction, there should be an equity share agreement, which includes an understanding of the terms of occupancy, possible buyout options, a property that suits each party's equity share needs, and a clear statement of who will be responsible for any necessary repairs and costs.

Equity share agreements may differ and will depend on the conditions that may or may not be unique to such an agreement. For example, if you are doing an equity share with an investor who puts up the down payment, your equity split could be less than the investor's share (e.g., 60%–40%). If you are a contractor or a handyperson and are occupying the property, the split could be based on how much work you are committed to doing. This could make up for the difference in investment and might give you an even split, even if the investor put up the money.

The equity split does not always have to be a 50–50 split; they will and should be determined by not only who put up the down payment, but who qualified for the loan, who is making the improvements, who is occupying the property, or who is making the payments to the mortgage company.

In an equity split, the persons occupying the property could be making the total payment each month. The investor in the meantime is able to share the benefits of the interest write-off; the equity partner living in the property can also enjoy a tax advantage versus throwing the money down a rat hole for rent each month. At the end of a perfectly executed equity share, both parties enjoy a profit, a tax write-off, pride of ownership in real estate, and eventually enough money to reinvest in another equity share, or other real estate opportunities.

AVOIDING PROBLEMS IN EQUITY SHARING

Understanding the advantages of equity sharing is easy when looking at such an opportunity at face value. Two parties come together, decide on a property, decide who will live in it, if not both, who will take care of it, how costs will be split, and how the equity will be shared. But let me explain some of the things to look for on the downside of equity sharing so you can be careful in making your decision.

Problems with equity sharing can sometimes end up in time-consuming arguments, if not expensive and unpleasant legal battles. Here are a few ideas to help you avoid an unfortunate situation.

The Involved Parties Should Create Their Own Equity-Sharing Agreement

Many equity-sharing partners or owners do not like to be involved in creating this agreement because the procedure is time-consuming and the real estate verbiage can be confusing. Don't rely on the owner to put together the agreement through his or her attorney. This approach to equity-sharing agreements is a mistake and should be reevaluated. The proper way to handle an equity-sharing agreement is to have both partners in the transaction meet with an equity-sharing or real estate attorney who specializes in equity sharing, discuss the basic issues, draft an agreement, and then review same to see whether it is acceptable to all parties involved. Once the draft is executed, make sure you read it thoroughly and understand its contents. If the wording does not make sense to you or you do not comprehend any part of the agreement, find out what you need to know to make the agreement clear in your mind. Although this process may seem frustrating and time-consuming, it will prepare you to solve future problems in an organized and rational manner, through discussion and compromise. If you understand all the provisions of the equity-sharing agreement, you will be better equipped to analyze any problem or unforeseen circumstances that may arise.

If you have a problem meeting with your equity partner, use a mediator to help you straighten out whatever needs to be resolved. Try to stay away from using attorneys for equity-sharing agreement problems; attorneys will be an added expense and it is possible to resolve problems without their help.

Watch Out for Default Risk

Most equity sharing owners understand the primary risks of the transactions in which they are entering; for the investor, a potential loss (down payment, time, and costs) and for the occupier of the property, loss of the home. But the greater loss is that credit problems may appear on the owner's credit report for the next seven years, along with the inability to finance future real estate and cars, obtain credit cards, and so forth. This is something that you, as an equity-sharing partner, will want to give some thought to.

To avoid the obvious, screen your equity partner on your own. Check the names and addresses of your potential partner's last two landlords (to verify how and whether rent was paid on time) and current and previous employers. Don't be intimidated to look at your partner's credit report or copies of tax returns and bank statements. This should give you an idea of spending habits and whether or not you want this individual as an equity partner. Now, if you are the one looking for an investor, don't be surprised if the investor requests the same of you.

Keep the Lines of Communication Open

To prevent an equity-sharing agreement from falling apart, you, as an investor, should always know whether there are any financial or maintenance problems. The occupier should mail copies of all bills being paid including copies of the checks for the mortgage, property taxes, and insurance. You can also ask the mortgage lender to notify you in the event of a late payment (beyond a grace period, or 30 days late), since you are on title. Although the lender might call the occupier directly, you could be out in the cold and totally unaware of what is going on.

As a safeguard, have your occupier set up a "reserve account" by making an initial deposit or paying a little more each month. If the occupier cannot make a payment, you can disburse the funds from the reserve account.

Finally, you need to be aware of problems that lead to default, such as the death of an equity-sharing partner. If you were holding title as joint tenants, you would have the automatic "right of survivorship." Since practically all equity-sharing investments are held as "tenants in common," the interest of the partner who dies must be willed. If there are many heirs, this could lead to a court battle, late payments, and so on. Make sure your equity-sharing partner agrees to put a will together when the equity-sharing agreement is made, and within a certain time frame. Also, check into the possibility of owner or mortgage insurance in the event of death. Many companies will pay off an interest in the property under a policy of this sort, and the remaining equity, although willed, will be there for the inheritor.

Keep in mind the motivation of the occupier of an equity-shared property. Due to the depreciation of real estate, the occupier might see it in his or her best interest to get out. Therefore, abandonment is something to watch out for.

When considering any real estate transaction, you should have a real estate broker or an attorney evaluate your contract. An equity partnership can be as close a relationship as a marriage. Be careful when getting involved. Make sure you know your equity partner well. If the person is a family member, a parent, or a close friend, you probably can gauge what the relationship will be like. On the other hand, if it's an investor, I am sure he or she will want to know just as much about *you* as you want to know about the investor. Be honest when entering this liaison.

6 REVERSE MORTGAGES: INCOME THROUGH HOME EQUITY

This chapter is a guide to home equity conversions based on information obtained from the American Association of Retired Persons (AARP). If you need any additional information contact the AARP at (202) 434-2277. The tables in this chapter illustrate accurate data provided by AARP. In the back of this book, you will find addresses and phone numbers of resources for further information on the programs discussed in this chapter.

Until a few years ago, the only way to get cash from your home was either to sell it, which meant a move on your part, or to qualify for a loan; you could borrow against your home but then would incur monthly loan payments. Now there are new and creative plans for getting money from your home called home equity conversions, which allow you to take cash from your home without having to move or repay a loan each month. Home equity conversions (HEC) are relatively new in the United States, but they have been available in European countries for some time.

This chapter will introduce you to the plans that are available and will describe the current HEC developments. I will

---

Information in this chapter was provided by the American Association of Retired persons (AARP).

explain how these plans work, give some examples of how they can be used, and will cover the advantages and disadvantages of the HEC. This information will help you determine whether the home equity conversion—among the options available to you—is the most suitable for your individual situation, goals, and resources.

Because home equity is such an important asset, you should consider home equity conversion plans within the larger context of your overall financial and estate planning. It might be in your interest to use a personal financial planner, attorney, or adviser before making this decision. Although various home equity conversion plans are similar in several ways, a review of the basic principles of home equity conversions will show you their similarities and differences.

Home equity plans are generally not free. When generating one of these plans, you could be charged application fees, closing costs, interest charges, sales commissions, or loss of future appreciation (future appreciation if your home goes up in value).

The cost of a home equity conversion plan can be very low or very high. The overall costs depend on how long you live and how much your home's value can change.

Home equity conversion plans use up your home equity (the value of your home minus any remaining mortgage or any other liens of record; e.g., if your home is worth $100,000 and you still owe $25,000 then you have $75,000 in home equity). This means the more equity you turn into cash now, the less you or your heirs will have later.

The more equity you have, the more you can convert to cash. If you have $100,000 in home equity, you will be able to generate twice as much benefit from a home equity conversion plan as a homeowner with just $50,000 in equity. If you are a renter, having no home equity, you will not be eligible for any of these plans. Home equity conversions do not create home equity; they will only allow you to use the equity you already have. Homeowners with a large outstanding mortgage are usually not eligible for this plan.

Like all real estate and financial transactions, home equity conversions involve some form of risk. In some plans, there is a risk you could have to sell your home and move. In other plans, a fixed monthly benefit might be enough to meet your needs now, but could fall shy of your future obligations due to inflation or unexpected medical expenses. Some plans use up your future growth in home equity appreciation, which could be very costly in the long run.

Although there are ways to reduce, eliminate, or insure against risk, these methods usually mean higher fees or lower benefits. The most important safeguard against future risks involved in home equity conversion is to understand how the plans work, and to select the plan and plan features that will best suit your individual needs.

The basic types of home equity conversion plans are as follows:

1. Special purpose loans:

    Deferred payment loan.

    Property tax deferral.

2. Reverse mortgages (RMs):

    FHA-insured RM.

    Lender-insured RM.

    Uninsured RM.

These two categories are loan programs. The sale plans include only two types:

1. Sale leaseback.
2. Life estate.

The basic types of home equity conversions differ from each other in many ways. Some of these plans are offered by private sector institutions, such as banks or savings and loan associations, or mortgage companies. Other plans are provided by the public sector through state and local government agencies and programs. Nonprofit organizations have also helped in the creation of these plans through counseling.

Home equity conversion plans can be categorized according to their benefits. Some plans offer cash that you can use for the purpose of your choice. Others provide benefits that you must use for specific purposes such as paying property taxes or making home improvements. These plans also differ in the timing and amount of their benefits. Some plans provide monthly benefits for a fixed number of years, others for as long as you remain in your home. The monthly payments remain the same in some plans; they can increase in others. Some plans permit you to take out a large lump sum of cash or to make irregular withdrawals from your home equity line.

Some home equity conversion plans involve borrowing against home equity, whereas others are based on selling home equity. As indicated by the preceding list, there are more loan plans than there are sale plans. Special purpose loans must be used in a specific way; in the reverse mortgage plans, the loan against equity can be used for any purpose.

The home equity conversion plans described in this chapter should not be confused with the various "home equity loans" and "home equity lines of credit" that are being widely advertised by mortgage lenders. Although both use the words "home equity," there are basic differences between conversion plans and home equity loans, the most important being that you must make regular monthly payments on a home equity loan. This means that the lender will require that you have a monthly income great enough to make the payments. If your income is not high enough, you will not qualify for the loan. And, if you do qualify and take out a home equity loan but fail to make the monthly payments, the lender can foreclose on you and you could even be forced to sell your home.

With a home equity conversion loan plan (either special purpose or RM), you do not have to make monthly loan payments.

This means that the lender is not looking to your income for repayment of the debt and will not disqualify you on the basis of not having enough income. Since you do not have to make monthly payments, you cannot default on a home equity conversion loan plan due to missed payments.

SPECIAL PURPOSE LOANS

The most widely available and most often used HEC plans are the "special purpose loans." These loans have to be used for specific purposes such as home repairs or property tax payments. But they do not have to be repaid until you die, move, or sell your home. Special purpose loans are usually offered by government agencies or private nonprofit organizations. Currently, there are two basic types of special purpose loans: deferred payment loans for home repairs and improvement, and property tax deferral loans.

The simplest type of HEC plan is the deferred payment loan (DPL). A DPL carries a very low interest rate. You do have to pay back a DPL until you die, move, or sell your home. Your repayment obligation is deferred for as long as you live in your home.

DPLs are most often made by local government agencies, and yet all such programs do not operate in exactly the same manner. In some programs, part or all of your loan is forgiven based on the number of years you live in your home after you take out the loan. The longer you stay, the less you pay. There are also limitations on who is eligible and what type of repairs and improvements can be made with the loan.

Most programs have eligibility requirements. Often your income and assets must be below certain levels. There may also be limits on the value or location of your home. If you have a substantial mortgage or other lien obligations against your home, you may not qualify. In some programs, there is a minimum age or limit on multifamily dwellings.

Assuming you qualify, what could you do with a DPL? In most programs you can use it for repairs and improvements that make your home safer, sounder, more accessible or usable, or more energy efficient. As a general rule, you can use a DPL to correct physical problems or to make your home a better place for you to live. Keep in mind that you cannot usually use one simply to improve your home's interior or exterior appearance; cosmetic changes are not ordinarily permitted.

The specific types of repairs and improvements generally allowed in DPL programs include repairing or replacing a roof, stairs, floors, porches, plumbing, electrical wiring, or heating equipment; installing insulation, storm windows, weatherstripping, ramps, rails, or handicap necessities (widening doorways, etc.)

ADVANTAGES AND DISADVANTAGES OF THE DEFERRED PAYMENT LOAN PROGRAM

The advantages of a DPL make it a very attractive loan. It is generally offered by a public agency at a zero or very low interest rate with no loan fees or "points" and with no repayment required for as long as you live in your home. The types of repair allowed in these programs often increase the value of your home. Improvements in kitchens and bathrooms, for example, can boost the future sales value of your property, and with zero interest, the loan may eventually pay for itself.

Not all repairs and improvements increase the value of a home, and some improvements might even decrease it. But a DPL is often a good investment as well as a good loan.

There are concerns related to the deferred payment loan program, assuming you can find and qualify for one. Though a DPL is one of the best loans you will ever encounter, it is still a loan. You need to consider whether or not you really need one. How important is the repair or improvement? Do the DPL program rules allow you to make the type of repairs or improvements you want or need? How much longer do you intend to stay in the home? Would a DPL against your property make you ineligible for some other type of home equity conversion plan that you might need in the future? If you expect your heirs to live in your home, how would they repay the DPL on your death?

The major drawbacks of the DPL plan are availability and eligibility. As stated earlier, the DPLs are made by local government agencies or by private nonprofit organizations involved in housing or community development. Call your local city or community housing department or check with the Department of Housing and Urban Development.

PROPERTY TAX DEFERRAL PLAN (HOME EQUITY CONVERSION)

Perhaps the most widely available home equity conversion plans in the United States are the various property tax deferral or (PTD) programs operated by the state and local governments. These programs let you borrow money from the government to pay your property taxes. You do not have to repay this money until you die, move, or sell your home. In other words, you can defer or postpone paying your property taxes for as long as you live in your home. Your taxes are paid with the money you borrow; therefore you are a fully paid-up taxpayer and are not tax delinquent in any way.

All PTD programs are voluntary. Each year, you can decide whether or not you wish to defer your property taxes for that year. All PTD programs charge interest on the money you borrow. The most common interest charges on this money are usually between 6 and 8 percent. Unlike many other loans, PTD loans generally require no loan fees or points. They do put a lien on your home, however, that must be repaid with interest, when you move or sell, or when your estate is settled after your death.

PTD programs differ according to the type of agency that offers them, the manner in which the money is handled, the amount of money that can be borrowed, and the requirements for eligibility. In some states, you must file an application before paying your taxes. The state then sends a check directly to your local tax collector in your name, or it sends you a check made out jointly to you and your local tax collector. In other programs, you can file an application after you have paid your property taxes. In this case, you receive a check made out to you. It is often the practice in local PTD programs to credit your property tax obligation as "paid" without issuing any check, no matter how the specific mechanics of a program operate. In every case, however, they place a lien against your home to secure the debt that you now owe.

The amount of money that you can borrow through PTD is not the same in every program. Most programs allow you to borrow the full amount of your property taxes in any one year. Other programs place a limit on the total amount that can be borrowed against any home. This limit is generally some percentage of your home's value or the amount of equity that you have in your home.

You must be 65 years of age to participate in most PTD programs. In a few programs, there is a lower age minimum or no age limit at all. Most programs also require that your income be below certain levels, but the limits generally do not exclude persons of moderate means. In some states, eligibility is not limited by income at all. PTD programs normally restrict the amount of existing debt against a home. If you still owe a substantial amount on your mortgage or any other loan for which your home is pledged as collateral, you may not qualify for PTD.

Advantages of Property Tax Deferral

PTD is a simple and straightforward home equity conversion plan. Its main advantage is that it makes more cash available to you. If you choose to defer your property taxes, then you spend less of your current income on taxes and have more left to spend or save as you choose. If your annual property tax bill has been a particularly difficult one for you to pay each year, PTD offers you a new way to pay that may be more convenient. Instead of paying each year with cash from pocket, PTD allows you to pay when you sell your home or on your death, using the equity you have built up over the years.

PTD interest rates are generally moderate and fixed by law. You have the option to decide each year whether or not you want to defer your taxes. Although you are not required to make any repayment for as long as you live in your home, you can usually make full or partial repayment at any time without penalty.

Disadvantages of the Property Tax Deferral Plan

PTD is available in just over one third of the states. If you defer your property taxes, you will have less home equity in the future than if you do not defer them. If you defer your taxes every year and make no repayment, then the total amount you owe will grow each year.

How fast your debt will grow, and how much equity you will have left, depends on the interest charged by the PTD program and the future growth in the value of your home.

A PTD loan could limit your ability to borrow against your home for other purposes. And it could be that some other type of loan might fit your needs better. You could probably get more money each year from a reverse mortgage, but the cost would undoubtedly be greater. If you need to make a home repair or improvement, a deferred payment loan may be more appropriate.

REVERSE MORTGAGES

The most flexible and adaptable type of HEC is the "reverse mortgage." This HEC loan plan is called a reverse mortgage (RM) because it works much like a standard mortgage loan, only in reverse.

When you bought your home, you probably took out a standard conventional or government insured loan. You started with a modest down payment and paid monthly installments over a number of years; eventually, you became the owner of this property free and clear of any mortgage payments or secondary financing. Your regular loan made it possible for you to acquire ownership of your home and to build up a substantial amount of home equity over the years you've lived in the property.

To take out a reverse mortgage, you must already own a home free and clear of all debts, or owe only a minimum amount of money on the property. The RM loan is then paid out to you in monthly installments or on a line of credit basis over a number of years. You are not required to pay back any of the monthly loan advances or interest until the loan term is over. At that time, you must repay all loan advances plus interest. In most RMs, no repayment is due until you die, sell, or permanently move away. A reverse mortgage makes it possible for you to convert some of your home equity into spendable cash while you retain ownership. Table 6.1 compares a reverse mortgage and a forward mortgage.

The figures in Table 6.1 are based on the assumption that the forward mortgage borrower makes a $5,000 down payment and that the reverse mortgage borrower owns the home free and clear of all debt. In the forward mortgage example, you purchase a $70,000 home using a $5,000 down payment and a $65,000 mortgage loan. You pay back the $65,000 at a rate of $570.42 (principal and interest) per month for 30 years. The total of all your monthly payments is repayment of principal and $140,351 in interest. At the end of 30 years, you own the property free and clear of any debt. The amount of home equity you now hold is $70,000 plus all increases in value that have occurred over 30 years.

In the reverse mortgage example in Table 6.1, you begin with a $70,000 home that you own free and clear of any debt. You arrange to receive monthly RM loan advances of $459.17 for seven years (seven years is the average loan term for this type of RM). If you remain living in your home for seven years, the

TABLE 6.1

Comparison of Forward Mortgage to a Reverse Mortgage

	Forward Mortgage at 10% Interest for 30 Years	Reverse Mortgage at 10% Interest for 7 Years
Home value when loan is made	$ 70,000	$70,000
Homeowner's equity	5,000	70,000
Loan terms—principal advanced to borrower	$65,000 at purchase	$459.17 per month for 7 years ($38,570)
Repayment by borrower	$570.42 per month for 30 years ($205,351)	$56,000 at end of loan term
Total interest paid by borrower	$140,351	$17,430
Homeowner's equity at end of loan term	$70,000 plus 30 years of appreciation	$14,000 plus 7 seven years of appreciation

Source: American Association of Retired Persons, *AARP Guide.*

total amount advanced to you is $38,570 (84 months times $459.17 = $38,570). At that time, you sell your home and pay the lender $56,000 ($38,570 is principal and $17,430 is interest). You retain $14,000 in equity plus seven years' appreciation on the home. If the property appreciates 3 percent per year, your remaining equity would be $30,091.

Although there are different types of RMs, they share some common characteristics. First, all RMs are "rising debt" loans. This means that the total amount you owe (your loan balance) grows larger over time. When you receive your first monthly loan advance, you only owe that amount. One month later, the lender adds one months's interest on the first loan advance to your loan balance and sends you your second monthly loan advance or payment. One month after that, the lender adds interest on your previous month's loan balance to your second monthly loan advance and sends you your third advance or payment. Because you are not obligated to pay back any of the principal advances or interest until some future time, your balance grows at an ever-increasing rate.

Table 6.2 shows how interest is charged on a typical reverse mortgage. It assumes that the monthly loan advance is $300 and the monthly interest rate is one percent (1%). Each month, the loan balance increases by the regular advance plus interest: It first increases by $303.00, then by $306.03, and then by $309.09. Over a long period, the ever-growing nature of an RM loan balance produces a substantial amount of debt.

Table 6.3 presents the amount you would owe each year for 10 years on an RM that paid you $300 per month at one percent (1%) interest per month. After the first year, you would owe $3,843, of which $3,600 would be principal (12 monthly loan advances) and $243 would be interest. But after 10 years, you would owe almost $70,000, nearly half of which would be interest.

A second feature common to all RMs is that the amount of money that can be paid out in monthly loan advances is related to the amount of equity you have in your home, the interest rate on the loan, and the term of the loan. In general, the more equity you have, the greater your loan advances can be. If you have $100,000 in home equity, you will ordinarily be able to get twice as much as a person with $50,000 in home equity. Also, the higher the interest rate, or the longer the loan term, the

TABLE 6.2

Increases in Loan Balances on a Reverse Mortgage over Three Months

After Month	Last Month's Loan Balance	Interest on Last Month's Loan Balance	This Month's Loan Advance	Current Loan Balance (Amount Owed)	Monthly Increase in Loan Balance
0	—	—	$300.00	$ 300.00	—
1	$300.00	$3.00	300.00	603.00	$303.00
2	603.00	6.03	300.00	909.03	306.03
3	909.03	9.09	300.00	1,218.12	309.09

Source: American Association of Retired Persons, *AARP Guide.*

TABLE 6.3

Increases in Loan Balance on a Reverse Mortgage over a Ten-Year Period

Assuming: Monthly loan advance same as Table 6.2 = $300.00
Compound interest rate = 1% per month

At End of Year	Total of Monthly Loan Advances	Interest at 1% per Month	Loan Balance (Owed)	Annual Increase in Loan Balance
1	$ 3,600	$ 243	$ 3,843	$ 3,843
2	7,200	973	8,173	4,330
3	10,800	2,252	13,052	4,879
4	14,400	4,150	18,550	5,498
5	18,000	6,746	24,746	6,196
6	21,600	10,170	31,727	6,981
7	25,200	14,394	39,594	7,867
8	28,800	19,658	48,458	8,864
9	32,400	26,046	58,446	9,988
10	36,000	33,702	69,702	11,256

Note: Actual figures can vary depending on loan balances and terms when considering your own individual situation.

Source: American Association of Retired Persons, *AARP Guide.*

smaller the loan advances can be. These relationships are explained more fully later in this chapter.

A third similarity among RMs is that you can generally request that the initial loan advance at closing be substantially larger than the rest. You can use this initial lump sum, in most cases, to pay off any existing debt against your home, to pay the closing costs or any other fees on your RM, to finance a home repair or improvement, or to use in any other way you choose.

All reverse mortgages become due and payable when you die, permanently move out of your home, or sell it. Other conditions that could require you to pay off the loan differ in detail from one plan to another. But most plans include standard mortgage clauses relating to failure to insure, maintain, repair, or pay taxes on the home.

A fifth feature common to most RMs is that your legal obligation to pay back the loan is limited by the value of your home. This nonrecourse or limitation of liability provision means that the lender cannot require repayment from assets other than your home. A nonrecourse clause also protects your heirs and your estate against claims by the lender.

You keep the title to your home with an RM. The lender does not become an owner of your property; however, if you or your heirs fail to repay the loan when it becomes due, then the lender has the right to foreclose and force you to vacate the premises. Most RMs permit you to repay the loan at any time without penalty. This means you can decide to end the loan by repaying all principal advances plus interest before you die, move, sell the property, or reach the end of a fixed loan term that you had previously selected.

Advantages of the Reverse Mortgage

Specific types of RMs have their own advantages and disadvantages. These are discussed later in this chapter, along with more detailed explanations of different RM types.

In general, an RM allows you to convert some or all of your home equity into cash while retaining ownership of your home and benefiting from some or all of the future growth in the value of your property. With an RM, you can decide how much equity you want to turn into cash and how much you want to reserve for future use or for your estate. RM advances can be used for any purpose you choose; you can generally get more money from an RM than from either deferred payment loans or property tax deferral loans.

The loan advances for an RM are nontaxable and do not affect your Social Security or Medicare benefits. If you receive Supplemental Security Income (SSI), RM advances do not affect your benefits or eligibility so long as you spend them within the month you receive them; this is also the case for the Medicaid program in most states. The amount of any RM funds you keep beyond the month in which they were received is added to your liquid assets and may affect your eligibility for SSI and Medicaid.

The Disadvantages of the Reverse Mortgage

All types of RMs use up some or all of your home equity, leaving less for you or for special purpose loans. The interest rates are generally higher and are charged on a compound basis. Application fees, points, and other closing costs are usually higher as well. The interest on an RM is not deductible on your income taxes until you pay it, which doesn't happen until you pay off your total RM debt.

RM advances end when you sell your home or no longer occupy it as your primary residence. A lengthy nursing home stay, for example, could lead to a repayment requirement depending on the details of the reverse mortgage. Risks associated with reverse mortgages vary considerably depending on the type of RM.

TYPES OF REVERSE MORTGAGES

How do reverse mortgages differ? At present, there are three basic types of RMs: The Federal Housing Administration insured RM; the lender-insured RM; and the uninsured RM. They differ in when they must be repaid and the kind of loan costs charged. Table 6.4 presents this information in summary form.

All FHA-insured RMs provide a full range of loan advance options: monthly advances for a fixed term; monthly advances for as long as you live in your home; a line of credit plan that lets you decide the timing and amount of advances; and combinations of monthly advances and a line of credit. Lender-insured RMs provide one or more of these same loan advance options. The uninsured RM provides monthly advances for a fixed term.

TABLE 6.4
Three Types of Reverse Mortgages

FHA-insured reverse mortgage	Monthly for a fixed term or for as long as you live in your home: line of credit or monthly advance plus line of credit
Repayment of total loan balance is due	When you die, move, or sell
Loan costs include	Interest at a fixed or adjustable rate plus insurance premium and sometimes a servicing fee; origination fee; closing costs
Lender-insured reverse mortgage	Monthly for as long as you live in your home; line of credit or monthly advance plus line of credit
Repayment of total loan balance is due	When you die, move, or sell
Loan costs include	Interest at a fixed or adjustable rate plus insurance premium; origination fee; closing costs
Uninsured reverse mortgage	Monthly for a fixed term
Repayment of total loan balance is due	When the loan advances stop
Loan costs include	Interest at a fixed rate; origination fee; closing costs

Source: American Association of Retired Persons, AARP Guide.

FHA-insured and lender-insured RMs do not require repayment until you die, sell your home, or permanently move away. The uninsured RM must be repaid in full when its term of monthly advances is over.

You are ordinarily charged an origination fee and various closing costs on each of these RMs. In addition, insured RMs charge an insurance premium and either fixed or adjustable interest on the loan balance. Uninsured RMs normally charge a fixed rate of interest on the loan balance.

FHA-Insured Reverse Mortgages

The Federal Housing Administration (FHA) began insuring reverse mortgages in 1989. The insurance permits borrowers to remain in their homes for as long as they choose. Under this plan, you are not obligated to make any repayment as long as you live in your home. The insurance protects borrowers and lenders against the risk that the loan balance could become greater than the value of the home. By collecting an insurance premium on all insured loans, the FHA creates a reserve fund to cover any losses that occur. FHA-insured RMs offer the most complete and flexible array of loan advance options.

The basic choices include a tenure plan, a term plan, and a line of credit plan. A tenure or term plan may be combined with a line of credit wherein you may switch from one payment option to another at any time. The tenure plan provides monthly loan advances for as long as you live in your home as your primary residence. These payments do not increase or decrease, and they keep coming to you until you die, sell your home, or permanently move away. The tenure plan gives you a new source of monthly income on a regular and long-term basis.

The term plan provides monthly advances for a fixed term that you select at loan closing. Monthly payments to you on a term RM are generally greater than monthly payments to you on a tenure RM. The shorter the term you choose, the higher the monthly payments will be. When the term of monthly advances is over, the payments stop. You still are not required to make any repayment as long as you live in your home. But you no longer receive the extra monthly cash to which you may have become accustomed.

The line of credit plan is the most flexible one. It lets you decide when to request a loan advance and how much to request. For example, you could use it for a major home repair this year and then not use it again until a new need arises, possibly an unexpected health care expense or a special assessment on your home. You could even use it to pay off an existing debt on your home, thereby relieving you of a monthly loan repayment.

Combining a monthly loan plan (tenure or term) with a line of credit will no doubt be an attractive option to many considering a reverse mortgage. The combination gives you more income each month plus the ability to meet irregular or unexpected expenses as they occur. By reserving some of your home equity for future use, the line of credit also gives you some protection should you need to sell your home. If you do not reserve some of your equity, you could be left with little or no remaining equity after paying off your loan balance. Without other resources, this could make relocation very difficult, especially if you need to move because of health factors. Adding a line of credit to a monthly payment plan is an option that all reverse mortgage consumers should give careful consideration.

The future flexibility of the FHA program is unique and important. It permits you to change from one payment option to another at any time without incurring new loan origination fees or closing costs. The only cost is an administration charge, usually no more than $50. If you have a monthly payment plan, for example, you could establish an added line of credit or convert completely to a line of credit. You could switch from a tenure to a term plan, or term to tenure, or lengthen or shorten a term payment plan. If you have a line of credit plan, you could add a regular monthly payment or convert completely to a term or tenure plan. This flexibility may be particularly important for persons whose situations undergo significant change. Retailoring the payment plan to your circumstances may be of great value later.

The overall cost of an FHA-insured RM varies according to the lender and prevailing interest rates. It is expected that lenders will charge normal closing costs plus an origination fee equivalent to 1 to 2 percent of the home's value. The insurance premium has two components: an up-front portion equaling 2 percent of the home's value charged at loan closing, and one-half percentage point added to the interest rate charged on the loan balance.

If your home's value exceeds certain program limits, the origination fee and initial insurance premium will be reduced accordingly. Lenders may also charge a monthly servicing fee or include this cost in the basic interest rate.

Closing costs, the up-front portion of the insurance premium, and up to the first 1 percent of the origination fee may be "financed" with an initial loan advance. If the origination fee does not exceed 1 percent, you would not need to incur any out-of-pocket cost to set up this loan. Instead, you would pay any financed costs (with interest) when you die, sell, or move.

Interest charged on the loan balance may be either at a fixed rate or an adjustable rate. If the lender offers an adjustable rate, it must be based on an annual rate, and may not change by more than two percentage points in any one calendar year or more than five percentage points over the life of the loan. A lender who offers this annually adjustable rate may also offer a monthly adjustable rate with no annual limit on rate changes, but with a lifetime limit or cap set by the lender. Any changes in adjustable rate RMs must be tied to an independent index that cannot be controlled by the lender.

The impact of an adjustable rate on a reverse mortgage is different from its impact on a forward mortgage. On a forward mortgage, when an adjustable rate goes up or down, the monthly payment to the lender goes up or down. Most people prefer a fixed rate on a forward mortgage so that the monthly mortgage payment remains the same year after year.

On a reverse mortgage, by contrast, changes in the interest rate have no effect on the amount or number of loan advances. Your monthly advances or line of credit do not change because of increases or decreases in the interest rate. Instead, a change in an adjustable rate on a reverse mortgage causes the loan balance to grow at a faster or slower rate. In other words, the amount you owe becomes greater or lesser than it would have been without an interest rate change. A substantial rate increase, for example, would make your loan balance grow at a much faster rate.

At closing, it is likely that monthly adjustable rates will be lower than annually adjustable rates, and much lower than most fixed rates. This means that the rate used to calculate your loan advances is likely to be lowest on loans with a monthly adjustable rate. The highest payments to you will generally be on a reverse mortgage with monthly adjustable rates.

The specific dollar amount of your loan advances in the FHA program depends on four basic factors: (1) your age on beginning the program, (2) the value of your home, (3) the overall cost of the loan, and (4) the specific loan plan you choose. In general, the greatest loan advances go to the oldest borrowers living in homes with the highest value and the lowest loan costs. Table 6.5 is an example of a monthly loan advance on an FHA-insured tenure reverse mortgage at various ages and home values.

Table 6.5 shows how your age and home value affect the amount of FHA's tenure loan advances. It assumes an expected annual interest rate of 10 percent (including service charge), an origination fee of 1.5 percent, and other closing costs equaling another .75 percent. The monthly advances are the greatest for the oldest borrowers because their equity is expected to be paid out in monthly advances over the shortest period. In the case of couples or other joint borrowers, the age of the youngest borrower determines the amount of the loan advances. There is no separate payment schedule for joint borrowers.

TABLE 6.5

Monthly Loan Advances on FHA-Insured Tenure Reverse Mortgage at Various Ages and Home Values

Age at Inception of Loan	Home Value			
	$75,000	$100,000	$125,000	$150,000
70	$204	$272	$339	$339
75	262	350	437	437
80	340	453	565	565
85	449	599	748	748

Assumptions: Expected annual average interest rate = 10%; Area home equity = 24,875; Origination fee = 1.5%; closing costs = .75%.

Source: American Association of Retired Persons, *AARP Guide.*

Table 6.5 also shows that loan advances are greater for homes of greater value although the loan advances on a $125,000 home are the same as those on a $150,000 home. This is because the FHA program places a limit on the amount of home equity that can be used to determine loan payments. The limit varies by county and can range from $67,500 in many rural areas up to $124,875 in high-cost urban areas.

Because Table 6.5 assumes a limit of $124,875, the payments for the $150,000 home are the same as the payments for a $125,000 home. These loan limits usually reflect the maximum FHA loan amounts for the same area. So check with your home equity conversion lender for maximum loan amounts that FHA will insure.

Table 6.6 demonstrates that lower loan costs mean greater loan advances, and vice versa. Note that the lowest combination of loan charges (1% origination, $15 servicing, and $600 closing cost, at 8.7% interest) produces the highest monthly loan

TABLE 6.6

Monthly Loan Advances on an FHA-Insured Tenure Reverse Mortgage at Various Loan Costs

Origination Fee	Servicing Fee	Closing Costs
1.00%	$15	$ 600
1.75	20	900
2.50	25	1,200

Monthly Payment at Specified Interest Rate			
8.7%	9.2%	9.7%	10.2%
$363	$352	$340	$329
354	342	330	319
342	330	318	306

Note: These figures coincide with above interest rate, servicing fees, and closing costs respectively.

Source: American Association of Retired Persons, *AARP Guide.*

advance ($363). On the other hand, the highest combination of loan charges (2.5% origination, $25 servicing, and $1,200 closing costs, 10.2% interest) generates the smallest loan advance ($306).

The final factor in determining the amount of the loan advance is the specific payment plan selected by the borrower. Table 6.7 shows how the amounts differ according to the various payment options.

The line of credit figures listed in Table 6.7 increase over time by the same rate at which the loan balance is initially scheduled to grow. This means, for example, that the $37,600 initial credit line in this table will grow to more than $46,000

TABLE 6.7

FHA-Insured Reverse Mortgage Payments by Type of Loan Advance

Assumptions: Age of borrower = 75

Home value: $100,000

Area home equity limit: $124,875

Origination fee: 1.5%

Closing costs: 0.5%

Expected annual average interest rate = 10%

Monthly payments

Tenure	$ 352
Term	
5 years	801
10 years	503
15 years	412
20 years	372
Tenure with:	
$ 5,000 line of credit	305
$10,000 line of credit	258
$15,000 line of credit	212
Line of credit (no monthly payments)	
Initial credit line	$37,600

Source: American Association of Retired Persons, *AARP Guide.*

after two years. The amount available at that time would be determined by subtracting any line of credit advances made during the two years (plus interest) from this new line of credit amount.

The overall cost of these loans can be seen by combining all the loan costs into a single, annual average rate of interest. This total loan cost (TLC) rate assumes that the borrower finances all loan costs. It includes the origination fee, closing costs, servicing fee, insurance premium, and the interest charged on the loan balance. It also takes into account the nonrecourse nature of the RM, which means that you can never owe more than the value of your home no matter how long you live and no matter what happens to its value. When you apply the total loan costs to the advances received during the loan, it produces the total dollar amount owed at the end of the loan.

Table 6.8 makes the following assumptions: Age of borrower is 75, value of the home is $100,000, area home equity limit is $124,875, the origination fee is 1 percent, the closing costs are $750.00, and the expected annual average interest rate is 10 percent.

Table 6.8 shows that the total loan cost (TLC) rate on an FHA-insured RM is greater in the early years of the loan and decreases over its term. The reason is that the various loan

TABLE 6.8

Total Loan Costs/Rates on an FHA Tenure Reverse Mortgage
Annual Average Home Appreciation

At End of Year	0%	4%	8%
2	46.3	46.3	46.3
6	15.8	12.7	15.8
10	12.7	12.7	12.7
14	6.4	11.8	11.8
18	2.2	10.5	11.4
22	0.1	8.6	11.1
25	−1.0	7.6	11.0

Source: American Association of Retired Persons, *AARP Guide.*

costs are a larger percentage of the loan balance in the early years than later; the percentage also decreases over time. The overall loan costs are lowest when borrowers exceed their actuarial life expectancy and there has been little growth or appreciation in the value of their homes.

The FHA regulations require that borrowers must receive "adequate counseling by a third party" (other than the lender). The counseling is provided by public and private nonprofit agencies trained and certified by the U.S. Department of Housing and Urban Development (HUD). The information about home equity conversion that counselors must discuss with consumers includes, but is not limited to, options other than a (reverse) mortgage that are available to the homeowner (e.g., other housing, social service, health, and financial options). The counselors also discuss other home equity conversion options that are or may become available to the homeowner, such as sale-leaseback financing, deferred payment loans, and property tax deferral.

Financial ramifications or implications of entering into a home equity conversion are also discussed, and finally, the borrower must receive a disclosure that a reverse mortgage may have tax consequences, affect eligibility for assistance under federal and state programs, and have an impact on the estate and heirs of the homeowner.

FHA reverse mortgage insurance also protects you against default by lenders, which occurs when lenders fail to make loan advances as required by the loan documents. If lender default occurs, the FHA continues making the loan advances directly to you. The penalty to lenders for defaulting is steep; loss of all interest on the loan plus potential administrative sanctions.

Advantages of the FHA-Insured Reverse Mortgage

The FHA-insured RM provides a wide choice of payment options at closing and permits future modifications at little cost. The loans are backed by the full faith and credit of the federal government. No repayment is required until you die, sell your home, or permanently move away. The overall cost of the loan can be quite low when borrowers exceed their actuarial life expectancy and their homes experience low appreciation. Comprehensive consumer counseling is an important part of the program.

The Disadvantages of the FHA-Insured Reverse Mortgage

In most cases, this program involves greater loan costs than uninsured RMs and special purpose loans. The overall costs are ordinarily greatest in the early years of the loan. FHA-insured RMs generally provide smaller loan advances than lender-insured RM programs. For example, a 75-year-old borrower living in a $100,000 home could get about $350 per month on an FHA-insured tenure RM plan. The same borrower could get $450 per month on a tenure basis from a lender-insured RM program. An exception to this pattern involves payments to single borrowers in the FHA program.

The difference between FHA-insured and lender-insured RM payments is greatest if your home's value exceeds the FHA's area home equity limits. For example, a 75-year-old living in a $200,000 home could get about $440 from an FHA tenure RM. The corresponding figure for a lender-insured RM is about $900.

To check the availability of the FHA reverse mortgage program in your area, you should call the nearest HUD field office. The phone number of the National HUD office directory will be listed in the back of this book, under Agencies and Credit Repositories addresses and phone numbers (additional information lines).

LENDER-INSURED REVERSE MORTGAGES

"Lender-insured" means that RM lenders create their own RM insurance or "risk pool," rather than purchase RM insurance elsewhere. By collecting a type of insurance premium or "risk pooling charge" on all their RMs, lenders create a reserve fund to cover any losses that occur. In this way, borrowers and lenders are protected against loss if a loan balance grows to exceed the value of a home.

This lender-insured plan permits the borrower to designate a percentage of home equity at closing that always belongs to the borrower. It means you can mortgage less than the full value of your home, reserving the remainder for you and your heirs. For example, on a $120,000 home you could decide to mortgage 75 percent and preserve 25 percent. The most the lender could ever recover from your property would then be 75 percent of its value. Your 25 percent share would not be included in the mortgage. You would then retain $30,000 plus all the future appreciation (or minus the depreciation) on that amount. If your home value increased by 5 percent per year, for example, you would have a minimum of $48,000 in preserved equity, 10 years after closing.

The risk pooling charge is a fixed amount calculated at loan closing and the interest rate charged on the loan balance is a variable, or adjustable, rate that may change over time. ·

As currently offered by one multistate lender, this loan is similar in cost structure to the FHA program. It provides both monthly loan advances as long as the borrower lives in the home and an optional line of credit.

The fixed premium or risk pooling charge in the plan is 7 percent of the mortgaged home value at closing (7 percent of the equity you decide to mortgage). If you die before receiving this amount in cash advances, your estate is entitled to a proportional refund. The variable interest rate on this plan is 2.5 percent over the 10-year U.S. Treasury Securities rate and is adjusted annually.

Table 6.9 presents the amount of monthly loan balances for various ages and mortgaged home values. The greatest loan advances go to the oldest borrowers with the highest mortgaged home values. The amount of the monthly loan advances also varies by the number of borrowers owning the home.

TABLE 6.9

**Monthly Loan Advances for Single Borrowers Offered by
Lender-Insured Reverse Mortgage**

	Age	Monthly Advance
Home value = $ 80,000	70	$ 272
	75	359
	80	467
	85	597
Home value = $100,000	70	340
	75	450
	80	585
	85	747
Home value = $120,000	70	409
	75	540
	80	703
	85	897
Home value = $140,000	70	478
	75	631
	80	820
	85	1,046
Home value = $200,000	70	684
	75	903
	80	1,174
	85	1,494

Source: American Association of Retired Persons, *AARP Guide.*

Table 6.10 assumes the home is owned by a single borrower. For joint borrowers, the advances are approximately 60 to 80 percent of the advances for single borrowers (assuming that the loan advances do not depend on prevailing interest rates at closing, and they do not change during the loan). The overall cost of lender-insured RMs are determined principally by how long you live in your home and how much its value appreciates during that time. Table 6.10 presents the total loan cost rates on lender-insured RMs.

TABLE 6.10
Total Loan Cost Rates on a Lender-Insured Reverse Mortgage

	End of Year	TLC Rate
Annual average home appreciation = 0%	2	73.8
	6	21.7
	10	10.0
	14	2.9
	18	−0.5
	22	−2.3
	25	−3.1
Annual average home appreciation = 5%	2	73.8
	6	21.7
	10	16.0
	14	11.3
	18	8.3
	22	6.7
	25	6.0
Annual average home appreciation = 10%	2	73.8
	6	21.7
	10	16.0
	14	14.1
	18	14.1*
	22	13.4*
	22	12.8*
	25	12.6*

*Assumes projected national average home appreciation (CPI + 3%) also equals 10%. If projected appreciation equals 5%, for example, see TLC rates based on 5% appreciation (11.3% at 14 years, 8.3% at 18 years, etc.).

Source: American Association of Retired Persons, *AARP Guide.*

Table 6.10 shows that these loans are very costly if you live in your home for a short period. If you know you need income only for a short time, then an uninsured RM may be a more appropriate choice. Uninsured RMs are due and payable on a specific date, but they do not include insurance or risk pooling charges.

Lender-insured RMs can also be very expensive when homes appreciate at a high rate. A unique feature in the loan currently being offered by one multistate lender provides an exception to this general pattern. This feature limits the total amount due on the loan to the value the home would have if it appreciated annually by the consumer price index plus 1.3 percent (approximate rate at which homes have appreciated on a national average basis). If your home appreciates at a higher rate, this feature may substantially reduce the cost of your loan. The overall loan costs on a lender-insured reverse mortgage can be quite modest or even very low under other circumstances.

The longer you live in your home, the lower the TLC becomes. Also, the less your home appreciates, the lower the TLC will be. If you exceed your actuarial life expectancy, and if your home appreciates at a low-to-moderate rate, then the TLC on your loan can be quite reasonable. The range of potential TLC rates from the highest possible to the lowest possible is much greater for lender-insured RMs than it is for FHA-insured reverse mortgages.

Although the lender-insured RMs are not backed by the federal government, they offer some protection against lender default. A contractual safeguard provides that defaulting lenders lose partial interest on the loan.

Advantages of the Lender-Insured Reverse Mortgage

Lender-insured RMs provide monthly loan advances for as long as you live in your home. Optional line of credit advances are provided in some programs. No repayment is required until you die, sell your home, or permanently move away. The overall cost of the loan can be low when you exceed your actuarial life expectancy while living in the same home and it appreciates at a lower rate. Loan advances provided by lender-insured RMs are generally greater, in some cases much greater than loan advances provided by FHA-insured RMs. Lender-insured RMs permit you to mortgage less than the full value of your home, thus preserving home equity for later use by you or your heirs.

Disadvantages of Lender-Insured
Reverse Mortgages

These loans generally involve greater expenses than uninsured RMs and special purpose loans. Lender-insured RMs can be very costly in the early years of the loan or when appreciation rates are high. Higher loan costs mean that your loan balance (the amount you owe) grows faster, leaving you with less equity. Check with your local banks, savings and loans, and mortgage companies for availability of these loans.

UNINSURED REVERSE MORTGAGE
(HOME EQUITY CONVERSION PLAN)

The most basic type of reverse mortgage is the uninsured or fixed term RM. This loan is paid out to you in monthly cash advances for a fixed term (for a definite number of years that you select when you first take out the loan). At the end of the loan term, monthly loan advances stop and the full amount of the loan (the total of all monthly advances plus interest) must be paid to the lender. Ordinarily, this requires selling the home.

If you take out an uninsured RM, you must select the amount of the monthly loan advance and the length of the loan term. Table 6.11 shows loan advances for typical uninsured reverse mortgages including the largest amounts you could receive on a debt-free home based on values of $60,000, $80,000, $100,000, and $120,000 at loan terms ranging from 5 to 11 years, and at different interest rates. This table assumes that the lender would limit the total loan balance at term (amount due when advances stop) to 80 percent of the home's current value. If your home is worth $100,000, then the total amount due at term would be $80,000 (80% of $100,000 value).

Table 6.11 demonstrates three basic features of a term RM. First, the amount you can get from an RM depends on the value of your home. The table shows that the maximum monthly

TABLE 6.11

Maximum Monthly Loan Advances on Uninsured Reverse Mortgages*

	Years			
Interest Rate	5	7	9	11
$60,000 home ($48,000 loan)				
10%	$ 614	$393	$273	$199
12%	581	363	246	174
14%	550	335	221	152
$80,000 home ($64,000 loan)				
10%	819	524	364	265
12%	775	484	328	233
14%	733	447	295	203
$100,000 home ($80,000 loan)				
10%	1,024	656	471	332
12%	969	606	410	291
14%	917	559	369	254
$120,000 home ($96,000 loan)				
10%	1,229	787	547	398
12%	1,163	727	492	349
14%	1,100	671	442	305

*Based on loan balances at end of term equaling 80% loan to value, at loan origination.
Source: American Association of Retired Persons, *AARP Guide.*

advances for a $120,000 home are twice as much as those for a $60,000 home. Second, when interest rates are higher, loan advances must be lower. For example, the maximum monthly loan advance of a five-year RM assuming an $80,000 home and 10 percent interest is $819. But it drops to $733 with a 14 percent interest rate. Third, and perhaps most important, the length of the loan has a dramatic impact on the maximum amount of the monthly loan advance. On an $80,000 home at 10 percent interest, for example, you can get as much as $819 per month with a 5-year term, but only $265 per month with an 11-year term.

There are two reasons for the drop in advances. First, you are spreading the same amount of equity out over a longer period. Second, the longer the loan term, the more substantial will be the effect of compound interest. On a 5-year RM, you would receive more than $49,000 in principal advances and pay nearly $15,000 in interest. But on the 11-year RM, you would receive roughly $35,000 in principal advances and pay nearly $30,000 in interest.

Uninsured, fixed term RMs differ from all other RMs in that they become due and payable on a specific date (or if you die, move, or sell; if any of these occur before the end of the loan term). If you do not pay off the loan when it becomes due, the lender has the right to foreclose on you, forcing you to move. For this reason, it is very important to be cautious when considering this type of loan and to be certain that it meets your needs.

These loans are best suited for people who need more monthly income for a limited and definite period, and who intend or expect to sell their homes when that period is over. These loans are not suitable for persons with a long term or indefinite need for monthly income or for persons who expect to remain living in their homes for a long or indefinite period.

If you consider taking out an uninsured RM, you need to think about four basic issues: (1) how much money you need each month, (2) how many years you need the money, (3) how you will repay the loan when it comes due, and (4) how much remaining equity you will need after paying off the loan. You also need to keep in mind that each of these issues is related to the others. Table 6.12 presents four examples of how a term RM on an $80,000 home might be structured to meet different types of needs. In Loans A and B, the borrowers both select a 4-year term, but for different reasons. Borrower "A" is a recently widowed woman who no longer has the benefit of a modest pension her husband had received while he was living. Sometime within the coming year or two, she plans to put her home up for sale, move in with her sister and find a part-time job. In the meantime, she needs about $300 per month in addition for her everyday living expenses. Her uninsured RM tides her over while she makes a major life transition. Without the RM, she might find it necessary to sell the home before she is ready to do so or to accept a lower price than she might otherwise get. The RM gives

TABLE 6.12

Four Different Uninsured Reverse Mortgages on an $80,000 Home at 10 Percent Interest

Loan	Loan Term	Monthly Advances	Total Monthly Advances	Total Interest	Maximum Loan Balance Term	Remaining Equity		
						0% Appreciation	3% Appreciation	6% Appreciation
A	4 years	$ 300	$14,400	$ 3,364	$17,764	$62,236	$72,277	$83,234
B	4 years	1,000	48,000	11,212	59,212	20,788	30,829	41,786
C	8 years	300	28,800	15,420	44,220	35,780	57,112	83,288
D	8 years	400	38,400	20,560	58,960	21,040	42,382	68,548

her the economic peace of mind and the time to adjust to a new period in her life.

Borrower "B" is very frail and ill. Her doctors do not expect her to live much more than a year. She has a strong desire to spend her remaining time in her own home. To do so, however, she needs in home help that costs nearly $1,000 per month more than she can currently afford. A term RM is her alternative to selling her home and moving to a nursing home or apartment.

Both Borrowers A and B select conservative loan terms (4 years) that exceed the time they expect to need the monthly RM advances. They expect to pay off the RM before the end of the loan term. The actual amount of equity remaining in the home at expected loan payoff, therefore, is likely to be greater than the amounts listed in Table 6.12.

If Borrower A remains in her home longer than she currently plans and sells it just as the 4-year RM ends, she will still have $62,236 in remaining equity even if her home does not appreciate at all during that time. If, as she plans, she sells the home within a year or two, and if the home appreciates as expected, she will have more than that amount to start a new chapter in her life.

Borrower B is less concerned about preserving equity and more concerned about using her equity to spend her remaining months in her own home. If she lives well beyond medical expectations and remains in her home until the end of the loan term, she will have $20,788 in remaining equity if there is no property appreciation. If the home's value grows at 3 percent or 6 percent per year, then the remaining equity will be $30,829 or $41,786, respectively.

Borrowers C and D each select a longer loan term, 8 years. Both are in their late 70s and plan to remain in their homes for another four to six years. Each is on a waiting list for an apartment in a congregate housing facility, and neither wants to move until the apartment is available. In the meantime, each needs a monthly income supplement. Borrower C selects $300 per month and Borrower D selects $400 per month. Borrower

C's income needs are more modest, and she wants to preserve more equity for the future. Borrower D's current needs are somewhat greater, and she also lives in an area that is experiencing much more appreciation than Borrower C's area.

Advantages of the Uninsured
Reverse Mortgage

These brief examples demonstrate some of the advantages of the uninsured RM. It provides a fixed amount of cash each month for a fixed number of years. It is a flexible loan that can be adapted to fit a variety of situations and circumstances.

For persons with short-term but substantial cash needs, the term RM can provide a greater monthly advance than other types of RMs, and the borrower retains the benefit of all future appreciation. Most term RMs are offered by private lending institutions such as banks or savings and loan associations. But often a local nonprofit or public agency provides independent information and counseling services to interested consumers. These services are usually free of charge and offer comprehensive information on a variety of later life planning options in addition to home equity conversion.

Disadvantages of the Uninsured
Reverse Mortgage

The most important drawback to an uninsured RM is that it must be repaid by a specific date. It carries the risk, therefore, that you could reach the end of your loan term and wish to remain living in your home. If there is sufficient equity remaining in your home at that point, the lender may be willing to extend your loan into the future. But the lender is under no obligation to do so and has the right to demand repayment in full. If you are unable to repay the loan, you will most likely have to sell your home and move.

You can reduce the risk by using term RMs only for term income needs, by selecting a loan term that exceeds the term of your expected needs, and by reserving sufficient equity (plus any home appreciation) for anticipated post RM needs. But circumstances and expectations can change, and the best-laid plans can disappear. An uninsured RM could lead to a difficult financial situation or the loss of your home.

HOME EQUITY CONVERSIONS (SALE PLANS)

In most cases when you sell your home, you move out and the buyer moves in. But with a home equity conversion (HEC) sale plan, you continue to live in your home while receiving purchase payments from the buyer. These plans are much less generally available and usually more difficult to transact than HEC loan plans. The two basic types of HEC sale plans are the sale leaseback and the life estate.

SALE LEASEBACK

In a sale leaseback (SLB), you sell your home to a buyer, who then leases (rents) it back to you. You become a renter with a lifetime lease in the home you just sold, but the amount you now pay for rent each month is less than the monthly purchase payment you receive from the buyer. So you end up with more cash each month. In addition, you are no longer responsible for property taxes, insurance, major maintenance, or repairs.

The most difficult part of an SLB has always been finding a buyer willing to delay taking possession indefinitely. In the past, the tax advantages of owning rental property (income tax deductions for expenses and depreciation) have attracted few real estate investors to the residential SLB, and the 1986 Federal Tax Reform Law has made SLBs by lengthening the depreciation schedule. By restricting the use of "paper losses," repealing favorable capital gains treatment, and reducing the tax rates, the 1986 law has decreased the tax value of an SLB for most potential investors.

The likeliest SLB buyers will probably fall into three general categories: (1) investors who expect there to be substantial future appreciation in your property; (2) persons who are attracted to your home as a future retirement home for themselves and may view the purchase through an SLB as a retirement planning device; and (3) friends or members of your immediate or extended family who are motivated, in part, by wanting to help you remain in your home or to keep the home in the family. Such motivation will not be sufficient in itself, however, since the tax status of an SLB is dependent on its being a true business transaction entered into on a "for profit" basis.

Finding a buyer isn't the only difficult part of an SLB. You also need to retain an attorney who is at least familiar with SLB arrangements, and preferably has completed a number of them. Assuming you can find a buyer and an experienced attorney, you still have a lot of work to do. Now you must negotiate the terms of the SLB. You will normally have to reach an agreement with the buyer on three issues: the lease, the sale, and the financing on the sale. Because these otherwise separate transactions are interrelated, review the "full package" beforehand so you can see how well your overall interests will be served.

The terms of the lease are of particular importance to you. Your right to remain in your home for life will be best protected by a lease term that substantially exceeds your life expectancy or by a contract clause giving you the right to renew a shorter term lease, at your option, indefinitely. The initial rental rate and the ability of the new owner to raise the rent in the future will be key factors in determining whether or not the SLB will meet your ongoing economic needs. In particular, you should compare the monthly rent you pay with the monthly purchase payments you receive from the buyer.

As an example, if your rent is $500 and the buyer's monthly purchase payment to you is $750, then you will net $250 cash per month (in addition to no longer being responsible for taxes, insurance, maintenance, and repairs). However, if the rent goes up 5 percent per year, in 5 years it will be $638 (leaving you only $112 net cash per month) and in 9 years it will be $775 (leaving you $25 short of being able to pay your rent with your monthly purchase payments). On the other hand, you need to avoid a "bargain" rate of rent that might jeopardize the tax status of the transaction.

Normally, a market rate monthly rent will equal anywhere from .007 percent to 1 percent of a home's value; this amount can vary greatly depending on local real estate conditions. You should compare any rent proposal with other rents being charged on similar properties in your area. Additional lease items to be negotiated include the right to the subject property and the responsibility for utility payments and minor maintenance/upkeep. The responsibility of the new owner for paying property taxes, special assessments, insurance, and major maintenance repairs should be spelled out in the lease agreement.

The purchase price for the home is a central element in SLB negotiations. For tax purposes, it is important that the price fall within a "market range" that reflects what your home would sell for on the open market. If a leaseback provision were not part of the market price, the price for your home should fall within a range of prices that willing buyers and willing sellers would agree on. The exact price you settle on may depend to some degree on other factors in the overall agreement.

In most cases, the buyer will not pay you the full purchase price in cash. Typically, the buyer will make a cash down payment and then pay you the remainder in monthly installments. Because you are in fact lending the buyer the remainder of the purchase price, the monthly installment payments made to you will also include interest. As a lender, you will need to negotiate the terms of the loan you are making to the buyer. These terms include the down payment, the interest rate, and the length of the loan. The amount of the down payment and the length of the loan term are important factors in determining your long-term income security. What will you do when the loan term ends and you no longer receive a monthly payment from the buyer? How will you pay the rent? Should you make the loan term so long that you are very unlikely to outlive it? Or would that reduce the monthly loan payment too much?

One solution to this set of questions is to use the down payment to buy a deferred annuity contract from a life insurance company. This contract could be set up to provide you with monthly cash payments beginning in the month after you receive your last loan payment and continuing until your death. In this way, you could guarantee yourself a lifetime stream of monthly payments.

The cost of the annuity would depend on your age, when you buy it, and the date its payments to you would begin. In other words, the term of the loan, the amount of the down payment, and the cost of the annuity are all interrelated. You need a loan amount (home value minus down payment) and a loan term that will produce a monthly loan payment sufficient to pay your rent and provide the extra monthly cash you need. But you also need a down payment sufficient to purchase an annuity that will continue your monthly income after the loan term ends.

Additional issues are (1) the use of a variable interest rate on the loan; (2) the right of the buyer to sell the property; (3) the right of the buyer to pay off the loan earlier than scheduled. A sale leaseback is a difficult and complex transaction, but it is not impossible. With a willing buyer and an experienced attorney, you have a reasonable opportunity to reach an agreement that will serve your interest.

Advantages of the Sale Leaseback

The attractiveness of an SLB versus HEC loan plan depends largely on your own attitude toward debt and homeownership. If you have strong feelings against indebtedness of any kind, and you do not place much importance on homeownership or retaining same, then an SLB may be more suitable for you than an HEC loan.

Whereas you pay interest on most HEC loans, you earn interest on an SLB in two ways: on the loan you give the buyer and on the annuity or other investment you buy with the down payment. If your SLB is properly structured, you may also be able to exclude from your taxable income up to $125,000 of the capital gain you make on the sale of your home. Giving up some or all the maintenance and repair activities that go along with homeownership may be attractive to you as well. Some homeowners are interested in SLBs because they want to reduce uncertainty about the future. They are concerned about future increases in property taxes, insurance, and the cost of maintenance and repairs. Additionally, they might be pessimistic and simply wish no longer to be speculating in the future appreciation potential of their properties. An SLB allows them to trade in these uncertainties for a firm, contractual schedule of future rent and purchase payments.

Disadvantages of the Sale Leaseback

In addition to the time, effort, and difficulty involved in finding a buyer and an experienced SLB attorney, you are also faced with the risks inherent in a complex set of negotiations. If the agreement you reach with the buyer turns out to be defective in any of several ways, your future occupancy rights and income could be threatened. Even if your occupancy rights are well protected by the contract, you still lose some element of control when you give up ownership for "rentership." You are now dependent on a landlord for timely repairs and on a borrower for timely loan payments. You do earn interest with an SLB, but you no longer benefit from future increases in the value of your home.

If you are currently eligible for your state's property tax relief program, you are likely to lose your eligibility or some of your benefits if you enter an SLB arrangement. You could lose eligibility if the program requires you to be a homeowner or if your SLB income raises your total income above the program's income limits. You could lose benefits if renters are eligible for lower benefits than homeowners, or if benefits are lower for persons with higher incomes. Take particular care in considering the effect that SLB proceeds might have on benefits from Social

Security, Supplemental Security Income, and Medicaid. The interest, annuity, and any nonexcludable capital gain income you receive could subject part of your Social Security benefits to taxation. The SSI and Medicaid programs (which provide benefits to low-income persons only) count any interest or annuity payments you receive as income for purposes of determining your eligibility and benefits. Also, in any month that you receive such a payment, it will be counted as a liquid resource and could affect your eligibility.

LIFE ESTATE

In this type of HEC sale plan, you remain the owner of your home until you die. What you sell is the right to ownership on your death. In real estate law terms, you keep a "life estate" (ownership until death), and you sell the "remainder interest" (ownership that begins when you die). Because you retain ownership throughout your life, you do not pay rent. But you normally retain responsibility for property taxes, insurance, maintenance, and repairs. Life estates and remainder interests do not offer the same tax advantage as an SLB. In particular, the seller may not take the one-time capital gain exclusion, and the buyer may not take deductions for expenses and depreciation. The buyer of a remainder interest, therefore, is unlikely to be a private, profit-seeking investor. Instead, life estate plans are usually offered by nonprofit organizations such as hospitals, colleges, and universities. In most cases, however, these plans include some element of charitable donation: They do not pay you full cash value for the remainder interest, but ask you to donate all or part of the value of the remainder interest to the nonprofit organization in exchange for gift tax deductions. Most homeowners interested in getting money from their homes would find little to gain in such plans because their incomes would probably not be sufficient to take full or even partial advantage of the tax benefit.

7 THE "SHORT SALE" AND "PREFORECLOSURE SALE"

BUYING REAL ESTATE AT A DISCOUNT

The terms "buyer's market" or "seller's market" are often used to describe the current real estate market from the basic economic viewpoint of supply and demand. The prices for goods and services depend on supply and demand. When the supply of a commodity is up and the demand is down, the prices drop. When the demand is great and outweighs the supply, the prices rise.

The savings and loan industry, mortgage companies, and banks have one thing in common; they do not like holding foreclosed real estate because the longer they hold the property, the more money they lose in interest, deferred maintenance, sales commissions, damage, and so forth. Thus, the "short sale" seems to have come into play with many lending institutions.

Example. A married couple came to me to be prequalified for a home loan. The home they were interested in is located in the Las Palmas area of Palm Springs, California, one of the most prestigious neighborhoods in Palm Springs, and a very old one at that. Many movie stars, doctors, lawyers, and movie industry executives have been buying property in this area for years. My clients came to me with an offer pending of $150,000, obviously one of the better buys I had seen in years. The property appraised for over $200,000 and the note on the property when it went into foreclosure had a balance of over $190,000. The bank "discounted the note" to allow the property to turn over quickly to a qualified buyer. The bank's primary interest was in getting the property off their books.

SHORT SALE

Short sales are done with major banking institutions, such as Bank of America, that have their own real estate owned (REO) department. These institutions will determine the property value, and to turn the property quickly, may discount the property as much as 30 percent or 70 percent actual loan to value.

For a Fannie Mae or Freddie Mac owned property, the lender would expect much more information on the buyer prior to deciding whether to accept an offer. I have verified bank accounts and pulled credit reports (with my client's authorization) and have actually been requested by real estate agents to submit this information with the offer. If that doesn't sound like putting the cart before the horse I don't know what does, but they are serious about turning their properties within 30 days from offer to recording. This can make it tough on the lender, but if you are a cooperative buyer looking for a deal, suggest the option of a short sale with your real estate agent. Some real estate agents deal strictly in the sales of REO properties. These are bank foreclosures listed with real estate companies for quick turnover.

PREFORECLOSURE SALE

The "preforeclosure sale" is a completely different animal. This program, designed by HUD, was targeted for homeowners who are in a default position and are willing to work with HUD to sell the property before actual foreclosure takes place. In a successful preforeclosure sale, neither foreclosure nor conveyance of the property to the Department of Housing and Urban Development occurs. The defaulting mortgagor sells the property at "fair market value" (with certain adjustments, as approved by the secretary), which is less than the outstanding indebtedness at the time of the sale. A mortgagee is eligible to file a claim for insurance benefits after a successful preforeclosure sale if the sale and related actions were conducted in accordance with applicable HUD guidelines and all qualifying criteria have been met. (The mortgagee would be the lender who would regain any losses due to the preforeclosure sale, since the property is being purchased at a discount compared with what is owed against it.)

A mortgagor in default can apply for assistance in a preforeclosure sale prior to actual foreclosure provided he or she can prove a hardship and reason for the default. The following are allowable reasons for default:

1. Death of a principal mortgagor.
2. Illness of a principal mortgagor.
3. Illness of mortgagor's family member.
4. Death of mortgagor's family member.
5. Marital difficulties.
6. Curtailment of income (reduction of income of a borrower).
7. Excessive obligations—same income, including habitual nonpayment of debts.
8. Abandonment of property.
9. Distant employment transfer.
10. Neighborhood problem.
11. Property problem.
12. Inability to sell property.

13. Inability to rent property.

14. Military service.

Although the previous mortgagor has had a hardship, the advantage to you, as a buyer, is that usually you can pick up the property for less than what is owed on it.

Depending on current market situations and depreciation levels determining new loan-to-values, many people who have purchased in the recent past do not see the worth in holding onto a property when it is upside down (more is owed on the property than it is worth). This decision to pursue a preforeclosure sale should be given careful consideration. A deed in lieu of foreclosure is a bad mark for anyone on a credit rating, although it may have never actually gone into foreclosure.

In many cases, if you're thinking about buying a property that is in "preforeclosure," and make an offer, the seller or mortgagee who is negotiating the sale will want an appraisal (although not required with the offer) to support the declining value in the area.

I have worked with clients who attempted to buy a preforeclosure property but could not do so because the original buyers or mortgagors did not qualify for the HUD-assisted preforeclosure sale based on hardship; yet, they still qualified for the loan on the house in which they were living. Just because the value of a property goes down does not mean that the homeowner can go into default and apply for this type of assistance. Many are turned down.

8 HARD MONEY LOANS AND QUICK QUALIFIER LOANS

HARD MONEY LOANS

The term "hard money" almost describes itself. Hard money loans are those originated and funded by private investors to borrowers who would otherwise be considered a heavy credit risk by traditional lenders.

Home loans are basically graded as "A," "B," and "C" paper, based on the borrowers' creditworthiness. "A" paper loans are for those borrowers without a history of credit problems. "B" and "C" paper loans are for borrowers who have had some form of hardship in the credit arena and cannot qualify for a regular loan. Following is a breakdown of differences in "A," "B," and "C" paper loans:

- *"A" Paper Loans.* Borrowers cannot have more than (2) 30-day-late payments on a mortgage in the past 24-month period; no bankruptcies in the past 36 months.

- *"B" Paper Loans.* Borrowers are expected not to have any 60-day lates on 50.5 percent of the current credit report; no more than (4) 30-day late mortgage payments in the past 12 months and not more than six in the past 24 months; no bankruptcies in the past 24 months; loans to be no more than 75 percent loan-to-value.

- *"C" Paper Loans.* Loans to be no more than 70 percent loan-to-value; no bankruptcy in the past 12 months. An unlimited amount of 30-day mortgage lates are allowed for the past 24 months, two 60-day lates and one 90-day late in the past 12 months; 65 percent loan-to-value on cash-out refinances.

The hard money loans described as "A," "B," and "C" paper differ in two respects; as the credit report shows a poorer rating, the interest rate will climb in determining what grade of loan you will be able to qualify for. The worse the credit, the higher the rate and fees. I strongly recommend avoiding hard money loans to anyone who can stay away from them.

Most hard money loans are adjustable rate programs and start at rates as high as 12.5 percent with a 6 percent margin and an 18 percent lifetime payment cap. Hard money lending should always be a last resort, especially if you are purchasing a home and can find a house where you can negotiate with the seller for your own terms, assume someone else's loan, or get in on the lease option as explained earlier in the book.

Hard money lenders are sometimes in the business to bail out a desperate borrower, knowing that in the event of a default, they could possibly get the property. With a 65 percent loan-to-value, the risk falls entirely on the borrower, and if a default occurs, there's enough equity in the property for the hard money lender to foreclose, resell the home or units, and make a profit.

QUICK QUALIFIER LOANS

Many companies in the United States are now offering programs called the "easy qualifier" or "no income qualifier" loan. These loans are available to all borrowers who are willing to put down 25 percent or even 30 percent. At one time, the down payment requirements were as low as 20 percent; they went up as a consequence of the failed savings and loans.

The reason easy qualifier loans are attractive to certain borrowers is that although a credit report is required, the borrower who is self-employed and does not show the income needed to qualify on his tax returns, can apply for this loan without having to submit a tax return. The income used to qualify the borrower is the income indicated on his home loan application. No verification of employment, 1040, or W-2 form is required. Many employees in resort areas such as Palm Springs, California, make a considerable amount of tip income. This figure is not always disclosed on a tax return causing the borrower not to look "good on paper," even though he or she can afford the payment.

No income qualifiers are another way for a borrower to obtain real estate. The risk is on the borrower because of the large down payment required. The lender will require a credit report, a verification of deposit, and an appraisal on the property to determine the value.

9 THE ULTIMATE FIXER-UPPER LOAN

When you are out house hunting, how many times have you heard the saying, "It's a fixer upper"? This phrase states that the property you are going to buy has suffered from what is commonly called "deferred maintenance."

When you are debating whether you should take on the task of fixing up a deferredly maintained property, you need to determine just how much work is involved. A fixer upper might only need cosmetic upgrades—paint, carpet, landscaping—anything to make the property presentable again. On the other hand, this fixer upper could mean something much worse, such as a new roof, electrical problems, faulty plumbing, or structural damage.

REHABILITATION LOANS

The Federal Housing Administration came up with a program that became very popular in the 1990s; it is called an FHA Section 203(K) rehabilitation loan, and was designed with the ultimate fixer upper in mind. I will explain how this type of loan can assist you in purchasing a home in poor condition with a small downpayment, allowing you to finance all the repairs and construction costs.

There is no other program such as this, in that you can purchase a property deemed "unlivable" and turn it into the home of your dreams. The Title 1 home improvement loan is for upgrades only and that is where the two differ.

The Federal Housing Administration (FHA), which is part of the Department of Housing and Urban Development (HUD), administers various single-family mortgage insurance programs. These programs operate through FHA-approved lending institutions, which submit applications to have the property appraised and have the buyer's credit approved. These lenders fund the mortgage insured by the federal government; HUD itself does not make direct loans for home buyers.

The Section 203(K) program, which is in the Department's primary program for the rehabilitation and repair of single family properties, is an important tool for community and neighborhood revitalization and the expanding of homeownership opportunities. Since these are the primary goals of HUD, the Department strongly supports the program and its participating lenders.

Many lenders have successfully used the Section 203(K) program in partnership with state and local housing agencies and nonprofit organizations to rehabilitate properties. These lenders, along with state and local government agencies, have found ways to combine Section 203(K) with other financial resources such as HUD Home and Community Development block grant programs. To assist borrowers, some lenders have also used the expertise of local housing agencies and nonprofit organizations to help manage the rehabilitation processing.

The Section 203(K) program is an excellent means for lenders to demonstrate their commitment to lending in lower income communities and to help meet their responsibilities under the Community Reinvestment Act (CRA). Because HUD is committed to increasing homeownership opportunities for families in these communities, Section 203(K) is an excellent program to use in connection with CRA-type lending programs.

The objective of the Section 203(K) program is to enable HUD to promote and facilitate the restoration and preservation of the nation's existing housing stock. How does the Section 203(K) differ from other loans? Most mortgage financing plans provide only permanent financing. That is, the lender will not usually close the loan and release the mortgage proceeds unless the condition and the value of the property provide adequate loan security. When rehabilitation is involved, a lender typically requires the improvements to be finished before making a long-term mortgage. When a homeowner wants to purchase a home in need of repairs or modification, the home buyer usually obtains financing first to purchase the dwelling, then additional financing to do the rehabilitation construction. Often the interim financing (acquisition and construction loans) involve relatively higher interest rates with shorter amortization periods. Construction and swing loans, or bridge loans usually allow a term of one year. The Section 203(K) program was designed to address this situation. The borrower can get just one mortgage loan, at a long-term, fixed rate, or a competitive adjustable-rate mortgage to finance both the acquisition and rehabilitation of the property. Therefore, to provide funds for the rehabilitation, the mortgage amount is based on the "projected value" of the property, taking into consideration the cost of the home after the work has been completed.

To minimize the risk to the mortgage lender, the mortgage loan (the maximum allowable amount) is eligible for endorsement by HUD as soon as the mortgage proceeds are disbursed and a rehabilitation escrow account is established; at this point the lender has a fully insured mortgage loan.

ELIGIBILITY REQUIREMENTS OF THE SECTION 203(K) PROGRAM

Eligible Properties

What types of property are eligible? To be eligible, the property must be a one- to four-unit family dwelling that has been completed for at least one year. The number of units on the site must be acceptable according to the provisions of local zoning requirements. All newly constructed units must be attached to the existing dwelling. Condominiums and cooperative units are not eligible for this type of finance. Homes that have been demolished or will be razed as part of the rehabilitation work are eligible provided the existing foundation system is not affected and will still be used. The complete foundation system must remain in place. In addition to typical home rehabilitation projects, this program can be used to convert a one-family dwelling to a two-, three-, or four-unit family dwelling. An existing multiunit dwelling could be decreased to a one-to-four family unit. An existing house on another site can be moved onto the mortgaged property; however, release of loan proceeds for the existing structure on the nonmortgaged property is not allowed until the new foundation has been properly inspected and the dwelling has been properly placed and secured to the new foundation.

A Section 203(K) mortgage may be originated on a "mixed use" residential property provided (1) the property has no greater than 25 percent (for a one-story building); 33 percent (for a three-story building) and 49 percent (for a two-story building) of its floor area used for commercial (storefront) purposes; (2) the commercial use will not affect the health and safety of the occupants of the residential property; and (3) the rehabilitation funds will only be used for the residential functions of the dwelling and areas used to access the residential part of the property.

The Section 203(K) program can be used to accomplish rehabilitation and/or improvements of an existing one- to four-unit dwelling in the following ways: (1) to purchase a dwelling and the land on which the dwelling is located to rehabilitate it; (2) to purchase a dwelling on another site, move it onto a new foundation on the mortgaged property, and rehabilitate it; (3) to refinance existing indebtedness and rehabilitate such a dwelling.

For items (1) and (3), the mortgage must be a first lien on the property and the loan proceeds (other than rehabilitation funds) may be available before the rehabilitation begins. For item (2), the mortgage must be a first lien on the property; however, loan proceeds for the moving of the house cannot be made available until the unit is attached to the new foundation.

Eligible Improvements

What are the eligible improvements of the Section 203(K) program? Mortgage proceeds must be used, in part, for rehabilitation and/or improvements to a property. There is a minimum $5,000 requirement for the eligible improvements on the existing structure(s) on the property. Rehabilitation or improvements or improvements to a detached garage, a new detached garage, or the addition of an attached unit(s) (if allowed by local zoning ordinances) can also be included in this first $5,000. Properties with separate detached units are acceptable; however, a newly constructed unit must be attached to an existing unit to be eligible under the Section 203(K) program.

Any repair is acceptable in the first $5,000 requirement that may affect the health and safety of the occupants. Minor or cosmetic repairs by themselves cannot be included in the first $5,000, but may be added after the $5,000 threshold is reached. The following are examples of eligible improvements:

- Structural alterations and reconstruction such as repair or replacement of structural damage, chimney repair additions to structure, installation of an additional bath(s), skylights, finished attics and or basements, repair of termite damage, and treatment against termites or other insect infestations.

- Changes for improved functions and modernization, such as remodeled bathrooms and kitchens, including permanently installed appliances (e.g., built-in range and/or oven, range hood, microwave, and dishwasher).

- Elimination of health and safety hazards; including defective paint or lead-base paint problems on houses built prior to 1978.

- Changes for aesthetic appeal, elimination, or obsolescence, such as exterior siding or addition of a second story to the home, covered porch, stair railings, attached carport.

- Reconditioning or replacement of plumbing (including connecting to public water and/or sewer system), heating, air conditioning and electrical systems, installation of new plumbing fixtures, including interior whirlpool bathtubs.

- Installation of well and/or septic system. The well or septic must be installed or repaired prior to beginning any other repairs to the property. A property less than ½ acre with a separate well or septic system is not acceptable; also a property less than 1 acre with both a well and a septic system is unacceptable. Lots smaller than these sizes usually have future problems; however, the local Department of Housing and Urban Development (HUD) field office can approve smaller lot size requirements where the local health authority can justify smaller lots. Local health authority offices are usually in the county building for the county in which you live.

- Installation or replacement of roofing, gutters, and downspouts.

- Installation or replacement of flooring, tiling, and carpeting.

- Energy conservation improvements, such as new double-pane windows, steel insulated exterior doors, insulation, solar domestic hot water systems, caulking, and weather stripping.

- Major landscape work and site improvement; patios, decks, and terraces that improve the value of the property equal to the dollar amount spent on the improvements or required to preserve the property from erosion. The correction of grading and drainage problems is also acceptable. Tree removal is acceptable if the tree is a

safety hazard to the property. Repair of existing walkways and driveways is acceptable if it may affect the
safety of the property.

- Improvements for accessibility to the disabled; remodeling kitchens and baths for wheelchair access, lowering
  the kitchen cabinets, installing wider doors and exterior
  ramps, and so forth.

When basic improvements are involved, the following costs can
be included in addition to the minimum $5,000 requirement:

- New freestanding range, refrigerator, washer/dryer,
  trash compactor, and other appurtenances (used appliances are not eligible).
- Interior and exterior painting.
- The repair of a swimming pool, not to exceed $1,500. Re-
  pair costs exceeding the $1,500 limit must be paid into
  the contingency reserve fund by the borrower. The installation of a new swimming pool is not allowed.

Luxury items and improvements that do not become a permanent part of the real property are not eligible as a cost of rehabilitation. The following items, including their repair, are not
acceptable under the Section 203(K) program: barbeque pit,
bathhouse, dumbwaiter, exterior hot tub, sauna, spa, and
whirlpool bath, outdoor fireplace or hearth, photo mural, gazebo,
television antenna, satellite dish, tennis court, tree surgery, additions or alterations to provide for commercial use.

Cost effective energy conservation improvements under
the Section 203(K) program must comply with the following
requirements:

1. *Addition to existing structure.* New construction must
   conform with local codes and HUD minimum property
   standards.

2. *Rehabilitation of existing structure.* To improve the thermal efficiency of the dwelling, the following are required:

   (a) Weatherstrip all doors and windows to reduce infiltration of air when existing weatherstripping is inadequate or nonexistent.

   (b) Caulk or seal all openings, cracks, or joints in the building envelope to reduce air infiltration.

   (c) Insulate all openings in exterior walls where the cavity has been exposed as a result of the rehabilitation. Insulate ceiling areas where necessary.

   (d) Adequately ventilate attic and crawl space areas.

3. *Replacement systems*

   (a) Heating, ventilating, and air conditioning system supply and return pipes and ducts must be insulated whenever they run through unconditioned spaces.

   (b) Heating systems, burners, and air conditioning systems must be carefully sized to be no greater than 15 percent oversized for the critical design, heating or cooling, except to satisfy the manufacturer's next closest nominal size.

   (c) Smoke detectors: Each sleeping area must be provided with a minimum of one (1) approved, listed, and labeled smoke detector installed adjacent to the sleeping areas.

APPRAISAL REQUIREMENTS

To determine the maximum mortgage amount, the Section 203(K) valuation analysis consists of two separate appraisals:

1. *As-is value.* The property is appraised in its present condition. It reflects those benefits to be derived from legal

use of the property; repair requirements are not included in this as-is value appraisal; closing costs are included, but reflect the as-is value of the property.

2. *Value after rehabilitation.* The expected market value of the property is determined on completion of the proposed rehabilitation and/or improvements.

The lender may determine that an as-is appraisal is not feasible or necessary. The lender may use the contract sales price (on a purchase transaction) or the existing debt on the property (on a refinance transaction) as the as-is value when it is clear to the lender that this amount does not exceed a reasonable estimate of value. On a refinance transaction, when a large existing debt (first and secondary mortgages) suggests to the lender that the borrower has little or no equity in the property, the lender should always obtain an as-is appraisal on which to base the estimate of as-is value.

For a HUD-owned property (a property that went through foreclosure and HUD is seller), an as-is appraisal is not required and a direct endorsement lender may request the HUD field officer to release the outstanding HUD property disposition appraisal on the property to establish the maximum mortgage for the property.

The HUD appraisal will be considered acceptable for use by the lender if (1) it is not over one year old prior to bid acceptance from HUD and (2) the sales contract price plus the costs of rehabilitation does not exceed 110 percent of the "as-repaired value" shown on the HUD appraisal. If the HUD appraisal is insufficient, the lender may order another appraisal to assure the market value of the property will be adequate to make the purchase of the property feasible.

PURCHASE OF HUD-OWNED PROPERTIES

Home buyers (including investors) who purchase HUD-owned property can refinance the property using a Section 203(K) within six months of the purchase, just as if they had purchased the property with a Section 203(K) insured loan to begin with. Evidence of interim financing is not required. The mortgage calculations will be the same as for a purchase transaction. Cashback will be allowed to the borrower in this situation. A copy of the HUD sales contract and the HUD 1 (settlement statement) must be submitted to verify the accepted bid price (as-is value) of the property and the closing date.

ARCHITECTURAL EXHIBITS

The improvements must comply with HUD's minimum property standards and all local codes and ordinances. The home buyer may decide to employ an architect or a consultant to prepare the proposal. The home buyer must provide the lender with the appropriate architectural exhibits that clearly show the scope of work to be accomplished. The following list of exhibits is recommended, but can be modified:

- *A plot plan of the site.* This is required only if an addition is being made to the existing structure. Show the location of the structure(s), walks, drives, streets, and other relevant detail. Include finished grade elevations at the property corners and building corners; show the required flood elevation.

- *Proposed interior plan of the dwelling.* Show where structural or planning changes are contemplated, including an addition to the dwelling (an existing plan is no longer required).

- *Work write-up and cost estimate.* Any format may be used for these documents, however, quantity and the cost of each item must be shown; also include a complete description of the work for each item (wherever necessary). The rehabilitation checklist should be used to ensure all work is considered. A copy of this should be available to you by your local HUD office, or your approved Section 203(K) lender. This should be accompanied by a draw request form (HUD-9746-A).

Cost estimates must include labor and materials sufficient to complete the work by a contractor. Home buyers doing their own work cannot eliminate the cost estimate for labor because, if they cannot complete the work, there must be sufficient money in the escrow account to get a subcontractor to do the work. The work write-up does not need to reflect the color or specific model numbers of appliances, bathroom fixtures, carpeting, and so on unless they are nonstandard units.

The consultant who prepares the work write-up and cost estimate (or architect, engineering, or home inspection service) needs to inspect the property to assure (1) there are not rodents, dryrot, termites, and other infestation; (2) there are not defects that will affect the health and safety of the occupants; (3) the adequacy of the existing structural, heating, plumbing, electrical and roofing systems; and (4) the upgrading of thermal protection where necessary.

TERMS USED IN THE SECTION 203(K) PROGRAM

The following definitions will help you understand the process as the loan originates, rehabilitation takes place, and the loan closes:

Insurance of Advances. This refers to insurance of the Section 203(K) mortgage prior to the rehabilitation period. A mortgage that is a first lien on the property is eligible to be endorsed for insurance following mortgage loan closing, disbursement of the mortgage proceeds, and establishment of the rehabilitation escrow account. The mortgage amount may include funds for the purchase of the property or the refinance of existing indebtedness, the costs incidental to closing the transaction. The mortgage proceeds allocated for the rehabilitation will be escrowed at closing in a rehabilitation escrow account.

Rehabilitation Escrow Account. When the loan is closed, the proceeds designated for the rehabilitation or improvement, including the contingency reserve, are to be placed in an interest-bearing escrow account insured by the Federal Deposit Insurance Corporation (FDIC) or the National Credit Union Administration (NCUA). This account is not an escrow for the paying of real estate taxes, insurance premiums, delinquent notes, ground rents or assessments, and is not to be treated as such. The net income earned by the rehabilitation escrow account must be paid to the mortgagor. The method of such payment is subject to agreement between mortgagor and mortgagee. The lender will release escrowed funds on completion of the proposed rehabilitation in accordance with the work write-up and the draw request form (HUD 9746-A).

Inspections. Performed by HUD-approved fee inspectors assigned by the HUD field office or on the HUD accepted staff of the direct endorsement lender. The fee inspector is to use the architectural exhibits to determine compliance or noncompliance. When the inspection is scheduled with a payment, the inspector is to indicate whether or not the work has been completed. Also, the inspector is to use the draw request form. The first draw must not be scheduled until the lender has determined that the applicable building permits have been issued.

Holdback. A 10 percent holdback is required on each release from the rehabilitation escrow account. The total of all holdbacks may be released only after a final inspection notice. The lender may retain the holdback for a maximum of 35 calendar days, or the time period required by law to file a lien, whichever is longer, to ensure that no liens are placed on the property.

Contingency Reserve. At the discretion of the HUD field office, the cost estimate may include a contingency reserve if the existing construction is less than 30 years old, or the nature of the work is complex or extensive. For properties older than 30 years, the cost estimate must include a contingency reserve of a minimum of 10 percent of the cost of rehabilitation; however, the contingency reserve may not exceed 21 percent where major remodeling is contemplated. If the utilities were not turned on for the inspection, a minimum of 15 percent is required. If the scope of work is well defined and uncomplicated, and the rehabilitation cost is less than $7,500, the lender may waive the requirement for a contingency reserve.

The contingency reserve account can be used by the borrower to make additional improvements to the dwelling. A "request for change form" must be submitted with the applicable cost estimates; however, the change can only be accepted when the lender determines (1) it is unlikely that any deficiency that may affect the health and safety of the property will be discovered; and (2) the mortgage will not exceed 95 percent (owner occupant) or 85 percent (investor) of the appraised value of the property. If the mortgage exceeds 95 percent or 85 percent of the appraised value, then the contingency reserve must be paid down on the mortgage principal.

If a borrower feels that the contingency reserve will not be used and wishes to avoid having the reserve applied to reduce the mortgage balance after issuance of the final release notice, the borrower may place his or her own funds into the contingency reserve account. In this case, if monies are remaining in the account after the final release notice is issued, the monies may be released back to the borrower (or buyer).

If the mortgage is at the maximum mortgage limit for the area or for the particular type of transaction, but a contingency reserve is necessary, the contingency reserve must be placed into an escrow account from other funds of the borrower at closing. Under these circumstances, if the contingency reserve is not used, the remaining funds in the escrow account will be released to the borrower after the final release notice has been issued.

Mortgage Payment Reserve. Funds not to exceed the amount of six (6) mortgage payments (including the mortgage insurance premium) can be included in the cost of rehabilitation to assist a mortgagor (whether a principal residence or an investment property), when the property is not occupied during rehabilitation. The number of mortgage payments cannot exceed the completion time frame required in the rehabilitation loan assessment. The lender must make the monthly mortgage payments directly from the interest-bearing reserve account. Monies remaining in the reserve account after final release notice is issued or when occupancy of the property occurs (whichever is first) must be applied to the mortgage principal.

MAXIMUM MORTGAGE AMOUNTS AND EXAMPLE

The mortgage amount, when added to any other existing indebtedness against the property, cannot exceed the applicable loan-to-value ratio and maximum dollar amount limitations prescribed for similar properties under Section 203(B), which states FHA's maximum loan for a primary residence that requires no rehabilitation. The mortgage payment reserve is considered a part of the cost of rehabilitation for determining the maximum mortgage amount.

Maximum Mortgage Calculation

The value is defined as the lesser of:

1. The as-is value of the property before rehabilitation plus the cost of rehabilitation.

2. 110 percent of the expected market value of the property on completion of the work.

Principal Residence (Owner Occupant). The maximum mortgage amount is based on 97/95 percent of the HUD estimate of value in item (1) or (2).

Investment Property (Nonoccupant Mortgagor or Builder-Rehabber). The maximum mortgage amount will be based on 85 percent of the HUD estimate of value in item (1) or (2).

Escrow Commitment Procedure. A builder-rehabber who purchases an investment property, but intends to sell the rehabilitated property to a mortgagor acceptable to HUD, may qualify for a mortgage based on the loan-to-value ratio and maximum dollar amount limitations prescribed under Section 203(B) for a principal residence, provided the dollar difference between the maximum mortgage amount and the mortgage amount available to an investor is placed in escrow with the lender.

To allow for maximum owner-occupant financing when the loan is assumed (by an owner-occupant acceptable to HUD) and to avoid the extra cost for a new mortgage, the down payment requirements for the investor may be based on the market value of the property after rehabilitation. The difference between the down payment requirements for an owner-occupant and an investor would be retained in an escrow account. If the property is not sold prior to the 18th amortization payment of the mortgage, the entire escrow amount must be applied as a principal balance to reduce the mortgage amount to an amount available for an investment property.

A first-time home buyer (FTH) can assume the mortgage for no down payment. An owner-occupant who is not an FTH must provide a downpayment into the deal. Another investor could assume the loan by putting a 15 percent down payment into the deal. If the resale price is less than the appraised value of the property, the mortgage amount must be reduced so that the purchaser maintains a minimum down payment based on the acquisition price. If the resale price is greater than the appraised value, the purchaser must make a larger down payment.

Example Assume a builder-rehabber can purchase a property for $50,000 and the cost of rehabilitation will be $20,000. The builder-rehabber will have to put a minimum of 15 percent down payment ($10,500) on the acquisition cost of $70,000 ($50,000 + $20,000; sales price plus rehabilitation estimate). If the after-rehab appraisal shows the market value of the property will be $100,000 after the completion of the rehabilitation, then the mortgage for an owner-occupant who will assume the loan will be $95,000. The builder-rehabber will apply $10,000 to the escrow account and the loan proceeds will provide $25,000 ($95,000 − $70,000). When the loan is assumed by a qualified borrower, the total of $36,000 in the escrow commitment account will be released to the builder-rehabber. A first-time buyer could assume this mortgage with no down payment.

Cost of Rehabilitation

Expenses eligible to be included in the cost of rehabilitation are materials, labor, contingency reserve, overhead and construction profit, up to six months' mortgage payments, plus expenses related to the rehabilitation such as permits, fees, inspection fees by a qualified home inspector, licenses, and architecture and engineering fees. The cost of rehabilitation may also include the supplemental fee that the mortgagor is permitted to pay when the mortgage involves insurance of advances, and the discounts that the mortgagor will pay on that portion of the mortgage proceeds allocated to the rehabilitation.

Exemption of the Market Value Limitation

The Section 203(K) regulations allow for a waiver of the market value limitation; such requests must be forwarded to the Assistant Secretary of Housing—Federal Housing Commissioner, at the HUD Headquarters. Requests must include documentation that the following conditions are present:

1. The property is located within an area that is subject to a community-sponsored program of concentrated redevelopment or revitalization.
2. The market value loan limitation prevents the use of the program to accomplish rehabilitation in the subject area.
3. The interests of the borrower and the Secretary of HUD are adequately protected.

Solar Energy Increase

The mortgage is eligible for an increase of up to 20 percent in the maximum insurable mortgage amount if such an increase is necessary for the installation of solar energy equipment. The solar energy system's contribution to value will be limited by its replacement cost or by its effect on the value of the dwelling.

SEVEN-UNIT LIMITATION

HUD regulations and policies state that an investor should not be allowed to rapidly accumulate FHA-insured properties that clearly and collectively constitute a multifamily project. In general, a borrower may not have an interest in more than seven units in the same subdivision or contiguous area. HUD considers contiguous "within a two-block radius." HUD can determine that units in a neighborhood are not subject to the seven-unit limitation if the neighborhood has been targeted by a state or local government for redevelopment or revitalization, or the state or local government has submitted a plan to HUD that defines the area, extent, and type of commitment to redevelop the area. A restriction may still be imposed within a redevelopment area to prevent undesirable concentration of units under a single (or group) ownership. HUD will determine that the seven-unit limit is inapplicable only if the investor will own no more than 10 percent of the housing units in the designated redevelopment area, or the investor has no more than eight units on an adjacent lot.

INTEREST RATES AND DISCOUNT POINTS

These are not regulated and are negotiable between the borrower and the lender. The amortization of the loan will be for 30 years; however, provisions of the Section 203(K) mortgage are the same as prescribed under the Section 203(B) owner-occupied FHA loan.

MAXIMUM CHARGES AND FEES

The statutory requirements and administrative policies of Section 203(K) result in deviations from the maximum amount of charges and fees permitted under Section 203(B).

Supplemental Origination Fee

When the Section 203(K) mortgage involves insurance of advances, the lender may collect from the mortgagor a supplemental origination fee. This fee is calculated as 1½ percent of the portion of the mortgage allocated to the rehabilitation or $350, whichever is greater. This supplemental origination fee is collected in addition to the 1 percent origination fee on the total mortgage amount.

Independent Consultant Fee

A borrower can have an independent consultant prepare the required architectural exhibits. A borrower can also use a contractor to prepare the construction exhibits or prepare the exhibits themselves. The use of a consultant is not required;

however, the borrower should consider using this service to expedite the processing of the Section 203(K) loan. When a consultant is used, HUD does not warrant the competence of the consultant for the quality of the work the consultant may perform for the borrower.

The consultant must enter into a written agreement with the borrower that completely explains what services the consultant will perform for the borrower and the fee charged. The fee charged by the consultant can be included in the mortgage. Acceptable fees are $400 for a property with repairs less than $7,500, $500 for repairs from $7,000 to $15,000, $600 for repairs from $15,000 to $29,999, and $700 for repairs and construction of $30,000 or more. For this fee, the consultant would inspect the property and provide all the required architectural exhibits. State licensed architect or engineer fees are not restricted by this fee schedule. The architect and engineer fees must be customary and reasonable for this type of project.

Plan Review Fee

Prior to the appraisal, a HUD-accepted plan reviewer (or fee consultant) must visit the site to ensure compliance with program requirements. The utilities must be on for this site review to take place.

The fee schedule is as follows and may not be changed without HUD headquarters approval:

1. Initial review prior to appraisal

Cost of Repairs	Fee
Under $15,000	$100
$15,000–$29,999	150
Over $30,000	200

2. Additional unit review (two- to four-unit dwelling under the same case number), $50 per unit.

3. Additional review (reinspection of the same unit) $50.

When travel distance exceeds 30 miles round trip from the reviewer's place of business, a mileage charge may be applied to the preceding charges, including toll road and other charges where applicable.

Appraisal Fee

To process a Section 203(K) mortgage, two appraisals can be performed, an as-is value of the property, and an estimated market value of the property assuming completion of the rehabilitation. The maximum fee that a lender may collect for these two appraisals is 1½ times the amount permitted for a Section 203(B) proposed construction appraisal, as established by HUD. Currently, this means you will pay anywhere from $300 to $450 in the worst-case scenario; it could be less than that amount depending on the charges in the county in which the property exists. Appraisal fees differ from county to county.

Inspection Fee

These fees are established by the local HUD office, and are fees for inspection during the rehabilitation of the property. Fees for a minimum of five draw inspections will be allowed for inclusion in the cost of rehabilitation. If all inspections are not required, remaining funds will be applied to the principal after the final release notice is issued. If additional inspections are required by the lender to ensure satisfactory compliance with exhibits, the borrower or contractor will be responsible for payment; the lender, however, has the ultimate responsibility.

Title Update Fee

To protect the validity of the mortgage position from mechanics' liens on the property, a reasonable fee charged by a title company may be included as an allowable cost of rehabilitation. When the mortgage position is protected and is not in jeopardy, this fee may not apply. Borrowers may wish to obtain lien protection, but the fees must be paid by the borrower where such lien protection is not required to ensure the validity of the security instrument. The allowable fee should not exceed $50 per draw release. If all draw inspections are not made, monies left in escrow must be applied to reduce the mortgage balance.

THE STEP-BY-STEP APPLICATION PROCESS OF THE SECTION 203(K) PROGRAM

This section describes a typical step-by-step application and mortgage origination process for a transaction involving the purchase and rehabilitation of a property. It will explain the roles of HUD, the mortgage lender, the contractor, the borrower, the plan reviewer, appraiser, and inspector.

1. The home buyer locates the property of his or her choice.

2. A preliminary feasibility analysis is conducted. After locating the property, the home buyer and their real estate agent should make a marketability analysis prior to signing the sales contract (purchase agreement) and should determine the following:

    The extent of the rehabilitation work required.

    Rough cost estimate of the work.

    The expected market value of the property after completion of the work.

    If you are the buyer, you do not want to spend money for appraisals and repairs specifications (plans) to discover that the value of the property will be less than the purchase price or existing debt, plus the cost of improvements. This is why the feasibility study is so important.

3. The sales contract is executed. A provision should be included in the sales contract that the buyer has applied

for Section 203(K) financing, and that the contract is contingent on loan approval and buyer's acceptance of additional required improvements as determined by HUD or the lender.

4. The home buyer selects a mortgage lender. You can call your local HUD field office for a list of existing lenders or check the local newspaper for HUD-approved 203(K) lenders; they usually advertise the types of financing that they can handle out of their offices.

5. The home buyer prepares work write-up and cost estimate. A consultant can help the buyer prepare the exhibits to speed up the loan process. If a plan reviewer is the consultant, Item 7 can be skipped and the exhibits can go directly to the appraisal stage.

6. The lender requests a HUD case number. On acceptance of the architectural exhibits, the lender requests the assignment of a HUD case number, the plan reviewer, the appraiser, and inspector—all at the same time.

7. The plan reviewer visits property. The home buyer and contractor meet with the plan reviewer to ensure that the architectural exhibits are acceptable and that all program requirements have been properly shown on the exhibits.

8. The appraiser performs the appraisal.

9. The lender reviews the application. The appraisal is reviewed to determine the maximum insurable mortgage amount for the property.

10. The lender prepares a firm commitment application. The borrower provides information for the lender to request a credit report, verification of employment and deposits, and any other source for documents needed to establish the ability of the borrower to repay the mortgage.

11. The mortgage loan closing takes place. After issuance of the firm commitment, the lender prepares for the closing of the mortgage. This includes the preparation of the rehabilitation loan agreement. The agreement is executed by the borrower and the lender to establish the conditions under which the lender will release funds from the rehabilitation escrow account. Following the loan closing, the borrower is required to begin making the mortgage payments on the entire principal amount for the mortgage, including the rehabilitation escrow account that has not yet been disbursed.

12. Mortgage Insurance Endorsement is received. Following the loan closing, the lender submits copies of the mortgage documents to the HUD office for mortgage insurance endorsement. HUD reviews the submission and, if found acceptable, issues a mortgage insurance certificate to the lender.

13. Rehabilitation construction begins. At loan closing, the mortgage proceeds will be disbursed to pay off the seller of the existing property and the rehabilitation escrow account will be established. Construction may begin. The homeowner has up to six months to complete the work, depending on the extent of work; some lenders may require the work be done in less than six months.

14. Funds are released from the rehabilitation escrow account. As construction progresses, funds are released after the work is inspected by a HUD-approved inspector. A maximum of four draw inspections plus a final inspection are allowed. The inspector reviews the draw request form that is prepared by the borrower and the contractor. If the costs of rehabilitation exceed $10,000, additional draw inspections are authorized provided the lender and borrower agree, in writing, and the number of draw inspections is evidenced on

Form 92700, the Section 203(K) maximum mortgage worksheet.

15. Work is completed; final inspection takes place. When all work is complete according to the approved architectural exhibits and change order, the borrower provides a letter indicating that all work is satisfactorily complete and ready for final inspection. If the HUD-approved inspector agrees, the final draw may be released, minus the required 10 percent holdback. If there is unused contingency funds or mortgage payment reserves in the account, the lender must apply the funds to repay the mortgage principal.

THE SECTION 203(K) PROGRAM: SUMMARY OF ADVANTAGES

There is a secondary mortgage market for the Section 203(K) program. The Government National Mortgage Association (GNMA), or Ginnie Mae, permits these loans to be placed in pools with 203(B) loans. The Federal National Mortgage Association, or Fannie Mae, along with the Federal Home Loan Mortgage Corporation, or Freddie Mac, will also purchase Section 203(K) first mortgages.

The Section 203(K) loan program is not restricted to single-family residences. This program is designed for one- to four-unit dwellings and can be used to convert single-family units into multiunits up to four and vice versa. The program does not allow improvements to a condominium.

The Section 203(K) program allows an existing house to be moved onto another site. Release of loan proceeds for the existing structure on the nonmortgaged property is not allowed until the new foundation has been properly inspected and the dwelling has been properly placed and secured to the new foundation. At closing, funds would be released to purchase the site and the rest of the mortgage proceeds would be placed in the rehabilitation escrow account. The borrower would have the site prepared to accept the dwelling. The first release would be based on the improvements made to the site including the installation of the existing structure on the new foundation.

The minimum amount of rehabilitation is $5,000 for improvements and repairs for the property to be eligible for this type of financing.

The following are the eligible improvements acceptable under the Section 203(K) loan:

- *Structural alteration and reconstruction.* These include replacement of structural damage, chimney repair, additions to structure, installation of an additional bath, skylights, finished attics or basements, repair of termite damage. This program has been very helpful in areas such as in Northridge, California, after a devastating earthquake.

- *Changes for improved functions and modernization.* This can include the remodeling of a kitchen or bathroom, and will cover permanently installed appliances.

- *Elimination of Health and Safety hazards.* Examples are removal of defective paint surfaces and removal of lead paint (for houses built prior to 1978).

- *Changes for aesthetic appeal.* You might eliminate obsolescence by adding a bathroom to a four-bedroom one-bath house, or a carport to an existing home with no garage.

- *Reconditioning or replacement.* Plumbing, heating, or air conditioning problems are included in the Section 203(K) eligibility. Installation of well and/or septic system must be done prior to the beginning of any other repairs.

- *Roofing, gutters, and downspouts.* This category is allowed under Section 203(K).

- *Flooring, tiling, and carpeting.* This category is allowed under Section 203(K).

- *Energy conservation improvements.* These include new double-pane windows, steel insulated exterior doors, insulation, solar domestic hot water systems, caulking, and weatherstripping.

- *Major landscape work and site improvements.* Included are patios, decks, and terraces that improve the value of the property equal to the dollar amount spent on the improvements or required to preserve the property from erosion. The correction of grading and drainage problems is also acceptable.

- *Improvements for accessibility for the handicapped.* Acceptable improvements are walkways, widening doors, lowering kitchen cabinets, and installing exterior ramps.

A carport can be placed on the mortgaged property, provided it is attached to the existing dwelling and meets HUD's and local codes for minimum property standards.

All work is done within the time frames set by HUD and the lender, such as the six-month requirement, which allows the borrower to be in the property within that time. Another advantage of the Section 203(K) program is that your loan will close usually 60 to 90 days after the acceptance of the sales contract. Another advantage is that the FHA Section 203(K) loan gives you the option of either a fixed- or adjustable-rate mortgage. If you are not occupying the property as your primary residence and are purchasing it as an investment, the adjustable-rate mortgage will not be offered to you.

Investors can use the Section 203(K) program; this is an advantage to investors because the normal requirement for investors purchasing rental properties is a 25 to 30 percent down payment, and the Section 203(K) only calls for a 15 percent down payment. They can also sell the property (and obtain their profit using the escrow commitment procedure) to a qualified home buyer who assumes the loan.

The Section 203(K) work does not have to be done by a contractor. Although it might be best to hire a contractor, the work can be done by the borrower as long as it is done in a timely and professional manner. A buyer doing his or her own work can only be paid for the materials. Monies saved can be allocated to cost overruns or additional improvements.

An investor can purchase rehab, and sell a property under the escrow commitment procedure, and this allows for good profits when the property is purchased at a good price, rehabilitated, and sold at the after-improved value to an assuming borrower. A first-time home buyer can assume this type of loan with no down payment.

Other advantages of the Section 203(K) program are as follows:

1. A borrower can own up to seven properties under this program, but will obviously be considered an investor, which will mean the 15 percent down payment rule will apply.

2. The property can be a "mixed use" property. This allows for commercial use on a property that can be considered your residence, such as a building with a storefront; however, funds can be used only for rehab of the living areas of the building.

3. HUD-owned properties can be purchased under the Section 203(K) program as long as the property is advertised that it is eligible for financing with a Section 203(K) loan. If the property is purchased using other financing avenues, it can be refinanced within the first six months of the closing using a Section 203(K) rehabilitation loan.

4. The final advantage is that an energy-efficient mortgage or (EEM) is allowed under the Section 203(K) program in the following states: Alaska, California, Vermont, and Virginia.

10 THE MORTGAGE BANKER'S ROLE

When I first moved from real estate sales into the mortgage banking field, my broker explained mortgage banking as being that part of the bank where all the desks are, void of the tellers and vaults. The business of mortgage banking is to originate, fund, and record home loans. The mortgage banker originates home loans for customers and provides a variety of loan programs that standard banks or savings and loan institutions may not have access to.

When dealing with real estate agents and brokers, the mortgage banker solicits their offices as a source for new business. By providing realtors with current rate sheets, cost breakdown sheets for buyers, and seller net sheets, the mortgage banker is able to establish his or her own client bank. The mortgage banker also solicits builders and developers for new business. Experienced real estate agents will use the services of a mortgage banker or loan representative from a mortgage company to determine the best available programs for their clients. In turn, a mortgage banker should be competent enough to assist the realtor in explaining the purchase process to any buyer interested in real estate finance.

I will explain the purchasing process by breaking it down into eight easy-to-follow steps.

Step 1.   Prequalify for a loan with a lender in your area (e.g., a mortgage company, bank, or savings and loan). Prequalification entails receiving an estimate of how large a loan you are able to handle based on your available cash, monthly income, and debts. Eventually, you will still have to go through the application process at a later time, yet your lender can determine whether or not you qualify for a loan and, based on the information you have provided, will be able to tell you the exact amount that you would qualify for.

Step 2.   Obtain the assistance of a real estate agent in your search for a home. The sales commission on a home is paid for by the seller, so it costs you nothing to retain a licensed real estate agent to work with you in finding the property you're looking for.

Step 3.   Once you've found a property you're interested in purchasing, make an offer on the property. Your real estate agent will help you complete a purchase contract and receipt for deposit that discloses the address, sales price you're offering, a deposit (to show good faith), and signatures by the broker and prospective buyer. Your broker will present the offer to the seller in the presence of the listing agent representing the seller, and the seller will then accept the offer or make a counteroffer. If the counteroffer is acceptable to the buyer, the acceptance portion of the contract is signed.

Step 4.   Open escrow. Escrow is the impartial third party that acts between buyer and seller. (*Note:* In states that do not have escrow companies, attorneys are used.) Once escrow has been opened and the deposit has been entered into escrow, the buyer makes an appointment with the lending institution or mortgage company that had previously prequalified the buyer. *If your real estate agent insists that you use a certain lender, he or she is in violation of the Real Estate Settlement Procedures Act or RESPA.* You can *always shop* for the lowest rates and best program available.

Step 5.   Since you have been prequalified by the lender, the loan application process begins; during this process, the lender orders an appraisal on the property and credit report, and sends out verification forms of deposit, employment, and mortgage or rental ratings to determine credit worthiness.

Step 6.   While the lender is researching the preceding information, your escrow officer is ordering both a Preliminary Title Report to obtain clear title insurance and demands for payoff of any existing loans of record that might be against the property. Always use or select a reputable title company to insure against any undisclosed liens or encumbrances on the property you are purchasing. (*Note:* Title insurance protects the buyer and the lender against future loss of the home arising from past defects of record in the title of the property.) The escrow officer will also handle the proper prorations of various county and city taxes as well as any bond assessments (assessments for curbs, gutters, etc.).

Step 7.   Once the appraisal on the property is completed and the lender has received all other required verifications, a loan processor will process the information in proper sequence and submit the loan to their underwriting department; this is where the final decision to approve the loan is made. When the underwriter approves the loan, loan documents are ordered and sent to the escrow company or attorney for notorized signatures, prior to funding and recording.

Step 8.   Before escrow is closed, insurance is ordered; a requirement by the lender to protect the lender from loss, in the event of a hazard, such as fire. The escrow officer will prorate tax amounts to the day the property records; this will eliminate the possibility of the seller being overcharged and will protect the new buyer from the responsibility of any delinquent or future taxes. A Policy of Title Insurance describes the land, names the owner and shows the title as it appears on the public records. These policies are issued in connection with nearly all real estate transactions in California and most other states. Escrow officers should have or can readily obtain a brief descriptive binder about title insurance policies for you. Once your note is recorded in the county recorder's office for the county where your property is located, it is your responsibility to notify the respective tax assessors so that you may receive notice of all future tax assessments.

You now have completed an escrow, from start to finish, and the property is now in your name. As stated previously, the role of the mortgage banker is to originate loans. In the next chapter, I will explain in detail how to qualify for a home loan and discuss the "low down" and "no down" programs available to you as the buyer.

11 QUALIFICATION GUIDELINES FOR A HOME LOAN

With the exception of ratios, the requirements to qualify for a home loan are similar for the Federal Housing Administration (FHA), the Veterans Administration (VA), the Federal National Mortgage Association (FNMA, or "Fannie Mae") and the Federal Home Loan Mortgage Corporation (FHLMC, or "Freddie Mac").

The four basic criteria that lenders use to qualify borrowers for a home loan are:

1. Income.
2. Job Stability.
3. Cash Reserves.
4. Credit.

INCOME

Verifiable income, such as wages shown on your tax returns or W-2 forms will be the basis for figuring out any qualifying ratios. Other income can be used such as interest income, dividend income, income from spousal support or child support, and overtime, if you have earned it for a long period and can show that you will continue to receive it. The lending institutions will require the past two years of income history. If the borrower's employment history indicates he or she is in school or in the military during any of this time, the borrower can provide evidence to support this (usually college transcripts or discharge papers). A borrower must also explain any gaps of employment of one month or more. Allowances may be made for seasonal employment such as resort areas that are closed during certain months of the year.

To analyze the probability of continued employment, lenders must examine the borrower's past employment record, qualifications for the position, previous training and education; the employer must confirm that such employment is likely to continue.

A borrower who changes jobs frequently within the same line of work but shows increases in pay will still be considered favorably.

The lender must analyze the income of each borrower to be obligated for the mortgage debt to determine whether it can be expected to continue through the first five years of the mortgage loan. If the borrower intends to retire during this period, the effective income will be determined by the amount of retirement benefits or award, along with Social Security, and so forth. In most cases, borrower income will be limited to salaries or wages. Income from the following sources, provided it is properly verified by the lender, can be included as effective income:

- *Income from overtime and bonuses.* This must be verifiable for the preceding two years, with the employer confirming the probability of continued overtime and bonuses.

- *Part-time income.* This could be income from seasonal work, such as farm work, Christmas sales, umpiring for baseball games. As long as the income has been uninterrupted for a period of two years or more and is expected to continue next season, it can be averaged in.

- *Military income.* In addition to base pay, military personnel may be entitled to additional forms of pay income (variable housing allowances, clothing allowances, flight or hazard pay, and rations). Land proficiency pay is acceptable provided its continuance is verified. An additional consideration may be the tax-exempt nature of some of these items.

- *Commission income.* Commission income must be averaged for a period of two years and the borrower must provide all schedules of Form 1040 for the previous two years. Commissions earned less than two years will not be considered unless the borrower changed from a salary to a similar position with the same employer.

- *Retirement and Social Security income.* Such income requires verification from the source (former employer, Social Security Administration) or through federal tax returns. If any benefits expire within approximately a five-year period, this will be considered a compensating factor.

- *Alimony, child support, or maintenance payments income.* Income in this category may be considered if such payments are likely to be consistently received for approximately the first five years of the mortgage. The borrower must supply copies of the divorce decree or legal separation and must furnish supporting documentation (copies of 12 canceled checks, deposit slips, tax returns, or bank statements).

- *Note income.* A copy of the note must be presented to establish the amount and length of payment. The borrower must provide proof these payments have been made for the past 12 months. The term of the note should be for at least five or more years.

- *Interest and Dividends.* Interest and dividend income may be used provided documentation (tax returns or account statements) support a two-year history of receipt. This income must be averaged over the two years.

- *Other sources of income.* These include VA benefits, rental income, auto allowances, trust income, nontaxable income (disability Social Security).

JOB STABILITY

The second requirement for qualifying is job stability. Job stability is pretty well covered in the explanation of income; two years is a required minimum on the job or in the same line of work. A person who has had three jobs in the past two years, in three different fields of work, would have difficulty qualifying for a loan.

CASH RESERVES

The third thing the lender will require is cash reserves, or settlement requirements. The normal cash reserve requirement would be to be able to verify with the bank, or document the source for the funds to close escrow. On a FHA loan, with a small down payment, your total cash to close (figured by your lender in advance) should be verified by the use of a verification of deposit form sent to the bank by your lender. Conventional loans require the same verification; cash reserves can be taken from a 401(k), pension plan, or other sources. However, penalties may apply, so check into that before you take any money out of a retirement account. The lender will want to see at least two months' worth of payments remaining in the bank at the close of escrow.

Borrowing money from another property (taking out a loan on a property that is free and clear) is allowed when financing a new home, provided it is properly disclosed. The new debt should be listed on the loan application and will be used against the borrower in qualifying.

Cash reserves should be in the bank for at least two months prior to purchasing a home; if the funds have not been there for two months, the funds will be backtracked to find out where they came from. Many types of loans will allow gift funds from a blood relative. This takes away some of the pressure a buyer may face in obtaining the necessary "cash to close." I have worked with many newlywed couples whose parents provided a wedding gift (money for down payment and closing costs) to help the young couple on their new voyage into marriage. This is totally acceptable by all lending standards whether FHA, VA, or conventional financing.

CREDIT

The final step in qualifying for a loan is credit. Past credit performance serves as the most useful guide in determining the attitude toward credit obligations that will govern the borrower's future ability to pay. A borrower who has made payments on previous or current obligations in a timely manner represents "reduced risk." Conversely, if the credit history, despite adequate income to support obligations, reflects continued, slow payments, the lender will view a prospective borrower as a "risk."

Late or Slow Pay

When analyzing the borrower's credit history, it is the general pattern of credit behavior that must be examined, rather than isolated occurrences of unsatisfactory or slow payments. A period of financial difficulty in the past does not necessarily indicate a risk if a good payment record has been maintained since.

Derogatory credit must be reviewed and determined whether it was due to a disregard for, or an inability to, manage financial obligations or factors beyond the control of the borrower. The borrower must explain in writing any derogatory obligations that have occurred in the past two years, and the explanation must make sense.

Not all lenders may require a collection be paid prior to closing; however, unpaid court judgments *must be paid or satisfied.*

For borrowers who have established no credit in the past, regardless of the reason for same, the lender must develop a credit history created from rent verifications, utility payment records, or other means; however, neither the lack of credit history nor the lifestyle of the borrower may be used as a basis for rejection. Remember, to a lender, *no* credit is better than bad credit.

Recent Debts

The lender must ascertain the purpose of any recent debts as to whether or not those debts were incurred as a means to acquire a portion of the monies for the down payment or closing costs. The lender will also look for a projected increase in debt, such as a mortgage payment that is higher than the amount being paid in rent.

When this payment will increase considerably, the lender will pay particular attention to a borrower's ability to save, and how that borrower handles financial obligations.

Foreclosure

The normal procedure for individuals involved in a foreclosure is that the borrower is not usually eligible for financing for at least three years unless the borrower can prove the situation was beyond his or her control, such as the death of a wage earner, factory shutdown or a serious long-term illness. Extenuating circumstances such as these may grant the borrower an exception to the credit rule.

Bankruptcy

This will not exclude the borrower, provided it is at least two years old and the buyer has proof of having straightened out his or her financial affairs, establishing a new line of credit. If the bankruptcy is less than two years old, the lender may consider extenuating circumstances, such as those listed for foreclosure.

QUALIFYING RATIOS

Debt-to-Income Ratios

Ratios are used to determine whether the borrower can reasonably be expected to meet the expenses involved in homeownership, and otherwise provide for the family. *The lenders must compute two ratios.* The first qualifying ratios I will explain are for FHA loans as listed in the *4155 HUD Mortgage Credit Analysis Handbook.*

Mortgage Payment Expense to Effective Income. Total mortgage expenses (principal, interest, taxes, and insurance plus additional required payments such as homeowners association dues) should not exceed 29 percent of the gross effective income. A ratio exceeding 29 percent may be acceptable if significant compensating factors are presented. Typically, for borrowers with limited recurring expense, greater latitude is permissible on this ratio than on the total fixed payment ratio.

Total Fixed Payment to Effective Income. If the total mortgage payment and all recurring charges do not exceed 41 percent of gross effective income, the relationship of total obligations to income is considered acceptable. A ratio exceeding 41 percent may be acceptable if significant compensating factors are presented.

Other Considerations: Energy-Efficient Homes (EEH). Both ratios, housing and debt, may be exceeded by up to 2 percent when the borrower is purchasing or refinancing an energy-efficient home (EEH). These ratios then increase to 31 percent and 43 percent respectively. The local HUD office determines whether a property qualifies for the EEH designation. Original documentation attesting to energy efficiency will be required on resales.

Condominium Fee. With proper documentation provided by the utility company, that portion of the condominium fee that is clearly attributable to utilities may be subtracted from the mortgage payment before computing ratios.

Compensating Factors

The following factors may be used in justifying approval of mortgage loans with ratios exceeding the guidelines:

1. The borrower makes a large down payment toward the purchase of the property (10% or greater).
2. The borrower has demonstrated a conservative attitude toward the use of credit and shows an ability to accumulate savings.
3. Previous credit history indicates that the borrower has the ability to devote a greater portion of income to housing expense.
4. The borrower receives compensation or income not previously reflected in the gross effective income that directly affects the ability to pay the mortgage.
5. There is only a small increase (10% or less) in the borrower's housing expense.
6. The borrower has substantial cash reserves after closing—at least three months worth of principal, interest, taxes, and insurance (PITI).
7. The borrower has substantial nontaxable income (if not an adjustment made previously in the ratio computations).
8. The borrower has potential for increased earnings, as indicated by job training or education in the borrower's profession.

Exhibit 11.1 is a *worksheet for qualifying buyers* that most lenders will use when prequalifying their client.

EXHIBIT 11.1
Prequalification Worksheet

Gross monthly income   (A)   _____
Include: Commission, overtime, interest, etc.

Monthly housing expense

Principal and interest   _____

Taxes (1.25% of sales price)   _____

Insurance (.00375% × S/P)   _____

Land lease   _____

Second trust deed payment   _____

                              Total   (B)   _____

Other monthly debts

Installment loans (10 months or more)   _____

Charge cards (5% of balance)   _____

Real estate loans   _____

Other   _____

                              Total   (C)   _____

Total debt service

(B) _____ + (C) _____ = (D) _____

Qualifying ratios

(B) _____ ÷ (A) _____ = _____ %

(D) _____ ÷ (A) _____ = _____ %

The (B) divided by (A) line ending in a percentage would be your housing expense, which should not exceed 29% by FHA standards. The (D) divided by (A) line would be your total debt ratio, which would include all debts plus new housing expense, and is shown as a percentage. This should not exceed 41% by FHA standards.

Example. You're buying a home for $75,000 at the current interest rate of 9.5 percent with $5,000 as a down payment.

Loan Amount: $70,000

Payment (principal and interest) (PI)	$588.59 per month
Taxes	78.12
Insurance	24.43

Total Monthly Payment:
   Principal, Interest, Taxes,
   Insurance (PITI)
	$690.14

Your gross monthly income is $3,000; this would go in line (A) on your prequalification form. Your housing expense of $690.14 would go on line (B). Divide your housing expense ((B) on the qualifying form) by your gross monthly income ((A) on the qualifying form):

$$(B)\ \$690.14 \div (A)\ \$3,000 = 23\%$$

A 23 percent ratio falls well below the allowable 29 percent housing ratio you are allowed to have for qualification.

You, the borrower, have a $327 per month car payment but no other installment debts. Enter $327.00 on (C) and add (B) (housing expense) to get your total *debt service* $1117.14(D).

Housing expense	$690.14
Installment debt	+ 327.00
	$1117.14

$1117.14 total debt, (A) gross monthly
income of $3,000 = 33%

This second figure (33%) is referred to by the lender as the bottom ratio; 33 percent falls well below the 41 percent allowable by FHA standards. You have a great chance of qualifying for this loan provided you meet the other requirements (job stability, cash reserves, and credit).

The qualifications for a conventional loan are slightly different. Most conventional financing, other than the seller carryback, comprises bank or mortgage company originated loans underwritten by FNMA or FHLMC guidelines.

Qualifying ratios are still used but the ratios change according to your loan to value (based on your down payment). If you are qualifying for a 95 percent conventional loan, the housing expense (top ratio on qualifying form) should be approximately 25 percent and the total debt service; (bottom ratio on qualifying form) should not exceed 36 percent. If you are putting down 10 percent, your ratio can be acceptable up to 28 percent housing and 38 percent total debt service. The reason these ratios seem more stringent than the FHA programs is that they are. Loans with less than 20 percent down require mortgage insurance, and not only have to be approved by the lender you applied with, but by the mortgage insuring company (MI). These companies underwrite after the loan has been approved, much like a second signature. If the loan is uninsurable by the mortgage insuring company, the lender cannot loan on the property. Mortgage insuring companies are General Electric (GE), General Motors Acceptance Corp. (GMAC), and United Guarantee Insurance (UGI).

Mortgage insurance was developed to protect the lender against the borrower moving into a default position. In the event of a default, the mortgage insurance company reimburses the lender any monies lost (usually up to 25% of the loan amount). This allows the lender to offer loan programs with as little as 5 percent down, whereas banks usually lend up to only 80 percent of the sale price.

Mortgage insurance is added to your monthly payment and ranges from 3.5 percent to 5 percent depending on your loan to value. The less you put down, the higher your mortgage insurance premium will be.

In qualifying for a *VA Loan,* another form of government-backed financing, the Veterans Administration only goes with *one ratio,* total debt service. Your proposed housing expense, plus any and all revolving debt divided into your gross monthly income will show a percentage that should not exceed 41 percent. I have closed loan transactions for veterans that have gone higher than 41 percent, but there were compensating factors such as the ones listed previously in this chapter.

LOW-DOWN AND NO-DOWN FINANCING PROGRAMS

The Federal Housing Administration (FHA Loans)

The Federal Housing Administration was developed in the 1930s to help the first-time buyer obtain real estate with a minimum down payment. This government agency was developed after the Great Depression and has since been one of the most successful agencies the U.S. government has ever backed. FHA is the insuring body for the Department of Housing and Urban Development and has insured millions of home loans since its inception.

FHA loans require only a minimum down payment. If the sales price of the property is less than $50,000, FHA loans only require 3 percent down. If you are looking in the $150,000 price range, up to 5 percent will be required as down payment.

FHA loans usually have a lower interest rate than conventional loans and are a great source for first-time buyers. I have dealt with hundreds of real estate agents, and the aggressive realtors who are making money are dealing with first-time buyers and low-money-down programs. In the current economic condition, especially in California, the majority of buyers are looking for this type of financing.

Veterans Administration (VA Loans)

The Veterans Administration is a government agency that guarantees loans for borrowers who have served in the armed forces. Any veteran who has been honorably discharged is eligible whether the person served during a war period of not. Some veterans who have served in the Reserves also may be eligible. To find out whether you're eligible for a VA loan, send a copy of your military discharge papers (DD214) and the request form from your lender (1880 VA) to the Veterans Administration. A certificate of eligibility will be issued to indicate an eligibility figure.

The VA offers no-money-down programs up to $203,000 (1996 figures) and has programs such as the "VA NO NO," (no money down and no closing costs). This program allows the veteran to pay a $1.00 deposit to make the contract binding; this deposit can be refunded at close of escrow.

The Veterans Administration loan program or (GI loan) is also an excellent avenue for the first-time buyer. I have dealt with many veterans who received the training needed to acquire employment while serving in the armed forces. They're able to qualify for home loans without being on the job for two years because the military training is given a time consideration.

When applying for a VA loan, the veteran can include the spouse's income to qualify. If the veteran is buying a home with any other individual, both borrowers must be veterans and have entitlement to qualify for the loan. If a married veteran dies, the spouse has the rights to the entitlement.

California Veterans (CAL VET)

This is another way for California veterans of the armed forces to purchase a home with a minimum down payment. Many other states have similar programs (check with your local state agencies for available programs). In California, many veterans take advantage of CAL VET financing. The CAL VET loan requires a 5 percent down payment and is an adjustable-rate mortgage. If the property is sold, it can be assumed, but only by another California veteran.

Farmers Home Administration (FmHa) Loan

This program offers a loan that is available to the buyer with a zero down payment. Whether or not you are a farmer, you could still be eligible. The Farmers Home Administration guarantees their loans up to 90 percent in the case of default. These loans are limited to rural areas (population 10,000 people or less). There are limits to the income the family can have, and the FmHa charges a 1 percent fee for origination. Although the criteria for qualifying seems stringent, thousands of these loans are made each year.

Public Employee Retirement System (PERS)

The PERS loan is a new program that allows the borrower to obtain 100 percent financing by borrowing against monies in their own retirement account. As a rule, a 95 percent conventional loan will be applied for through an institutional lender or mortgage company and the 5 percent difference will be money borrowed from your retirement account.

The retirement account that you are borrowing against cannot exceed more than 50 percent of what you have in retirement. PERS sets the rate on the money borrowed which is usually in line with the current fixed rates offered by banks and mortgage lenders. The 95 percent loan can be fixed or adjustable, but the lender is limited to the amount of points that can be charged when the borrower is going through the PERS program. The discount points in this case cannot exceed more than 1 percent of the gross loan amount. This helps keep the closing costs and cash to close to a minimum for the borrower. The PERS loan is an attractive loan for the borrower who is looking for the maximum leverage and is interested in a good interest write-off.

Other Loan Programs

The Community Assistance Loan Program is a conventional loan that allows the borrower to come in with only 3 percent down and a 2 percent gift from a blood relative. This program helps the first-time buyer obtain financing without having to come out of pocket with a large down payment.

There are other state programs that require "low" and "no down" such as those offered by the California Housing Authority. This is usually money derived from bonds, such as Los Angeles County bonds, money put away for building freeways, bridges, and so forth, and made available to people buying homes, usually in a tract or development. Each state has these types of loan available. Ask your mortgage banker for further information on the availability and qualifying criteria.

FANNIE MAE FIRST-TIME BUYER

The Federal National Mortgage Association, commonly known as Fannie Mae, was formed in 1938. This is a private company that makes sure mortgage money is available for individuals in communities all across the United States. Their sole function is to make sure banks, savings and loans, mortgage companies, and lending institutions have money available for you as a home buyer; their only business is assisting lenders make mortgages.

When you want to purchase a home, you will be faced with many decisions, the first being whether or not you are actually ready to buy. Finding the right home is not always easy and getting a mortgage loan can be time consuming and complicated. To help you decide if you are ready to buy, I will take you through the steps a mortgage company or lending institution uses in deciding whether you qualify for a mortgage loan.

When you take out a loan, you sign documents that say you promise to pay back the loan. When a mortgage lending institution makes your loan, it has determined that there is a good likelihood that you can keep that promise. The mortgage lender knows that it does not help you or the lending institution if you receive a loan, but then, for any reason, are unable to make the payments each month. To decide whether you will be able to repay the loan, the lender will look at many different pieces of information about you. This process is called "underwriting." These pieces of information show how well you have repaid your debts in the past, whether you are likely to repay your debts in the future, and considers your ability to repay the mortgage and your current debts. Think of it this way—each loan package is much like a book; if there is a chapter missing, the book makes no sense. An underwriter would then raise questions and bring forward conditions to be met before rendering a decision.

There are some general guidelines that help a lender in looking at these pieces of information about you. But you should also remember that there is some flexibility in these guidelines because everyone's financial situation is unique. If you are very strong in one area, it may offset a weakness you show in another area. Before you decide to jump on the home-buyer bandwagon, you should ask yourself several questions that I will go over with you. After answering these questions about yourself, you will realize whether it is time for you to purchase or whether you need to spend additional time to improve your current credit history, pay off existing debts, or save more money.

How Steady Is Your Job History?

This is important! Having a steady job helps you keep your promise to pay back a mortgage loan. If you have been working continuously for two years or more, you are considered to have steady employment. A lending institution will need to know your job history, and it will be a major factor in whether you can qualify for a loan. However, you do not have to have held the same job for two years to be approved for a loan. Job changes that have resulted in equal or more pay and continue to use proven skills work in your favor when your loan is being underwritten. If you have been working continuously for less than two years, the mortgage lender will look for an explanation. For instance, you may have been discharged recently from the military or just finished school. Your work may be seasonal and there might be gaps between seasons, such as work in resort areas where there are high and low periods of activity. There may be other acceptable reasons why you have not been employed continuously for two years, too. For example, you may have been laid off because of a factory or plant closing, or an illness. Or you may be in a line of work in which frequent job turnover can be customary, but you have been consistently employed and have maintained a regular, consistent level of income. If you have been fired for cause such as excessive absences, have long gaps in your employment record or have dips in your income level that are difficult to explain, you should probably delay buying a home until you can demonstrate stable work history. As far as qualifying goes, remember you can use other means for homeownership explained in this text that do not require loan qualifying, (e.g., assumptions and seller financing).

Do You Pay Your Bills on Time Each Month?

How you have paid your bills in the past gives a lender some indication of how you can be expected to pay them in the future. When you apply for a mortgage, you will be asked to list all debts, the amount of your monthly payments, and the number of months or years left to pay on these debts. Your lending institution will order a full factual credit report to verify the information that you provide on your application and will check how well you have kept your promises to repay your debts. Credit reports are provided by credit reporting companies that make inquiries through a wide range of available sources of information such as banks that may have given you a car loan, credit card companies, even gasoline companies and department stores that offer credit cards. Make sure that you disclose all your debts and any difficulty you may have had in the past in repaying these loans. If you are straightforward and honest with your lender, it will make the process much easier for all concerned because eventually the truth will surface regarding your credit history, employment, and so forth. It is also important not to leave out any information about money you owe. Credit reporting agencies have access to a great deal of financial information about you, and they make it available to the lenders who will be reviewing your application. If you have previously owned a home on which the mortgage has been foreclosed within the past seven years, the foreclosure will be revealed on your credit report. Having a foreclosure on your records does not mean you can never buy another home. Your lender will want to know the reason for the foreclosure and most prefer that three years go by before you apply for a new mortgage (the same requirement as for FHA loans). If you have declared bankruptcy within the past 10 years, that also will be revealed on your credit report and it will be helpful for you to explain the circumstances surrounding it. Lending institutions prefer that you wait at least two years after the discharge of the bankruptcy before assuming the responsibility of a large debt such as a mortgage loan. This gives you time to reestablish credit and show that you are again able to manage your financial affairs.

Many times credit reports are inaccurate or give a misleading picture of past credit problems that have since been resolved. To check the accuracy of your credit report, you can obtain a copy either free or for a small fee. Chapters 14 and 15 of this book explain how to obtain copies of your credit report and correct any errors that may appear on it.

If your credit report divulges a poor credit history and the information is correct, you should probably delay trying to buy a home and take the necessary steps to improve your credit profile. For instance, you may have too many debts or you may pay some debts late each month. If so, you should work to bring your payments up to date and to pay off some of your existing debt. Even if your debts are current, you may not be considered a good candidate for a loan if you have made your monthly payments after the due date each month. After you have decreased the amount you owe and are able to show the two-year history of making payments on time, you then may be ready to qualify for a Fannie Mae loan and buy the home of your dreams.

If you have never had any credit cards or taken out a loan through a financial institution, the various credit reporting agencies may not be able to issue a credit report on you, at which time they will state "no trades developed." In this case, you may be able to use a "nontraditional" credit history by documenting how you pay your rent, utility bills, and other obligations on time each month. You can put these records together yourself by making copies of canceled checks or showing copies of monthly bills that do not have any late charges. Copies of money orders or cashier's checks may also be acceptable in proving creditworthiness. A mortgage lender should be able to guide you in putting this type of information together.

Have You Saved Enough Money for a Down Payment?

When you buy a home you will need money that you have saved for a down payment and "closing costs." The amount of the down payment may vary, but generally you must make a down payment that equals at least 5 percent of the purchase price. (Fannie Mac and Freddie Mac seller-"owned" properties require 3% down). You will also need money for closing costs. These costs can be expensive, depending where you live. Sometimes, the property seller is willing to pay part of your closing costs.

The mortgage lending institution will want proof that you have saved the funds that you will use for a down payment and part or all of the closing costs. If the funds are in a savings account, the lender will ask the financial institution holding those funds to verify the amount and the length of time that the funds have been in your account. *The lender wants to make sure that you are not borrowing all the money you will use for the down payment and closing costs.*

Some communities have programs to assist the first-time home buyer; with some of these programs, you may be able to accept a *gift* from a relative or to borrow a portion of the money you will need for the down payment and closing costs from a local nonprofit organization or government agency. With others, you may be able to get a grant or other funds that you will not have to repay and can use to cover some of these costs. For assistance in down payment, refer to PERS Loans (Public Employee Retirement Systems) or city employer assistance programs provided by FHA-backed loans.

If you do not now have at least a portion of the money saved, this probably is not the right time for you to try to buy a home. Instead, it would be a good idea to open a savings account and begin putting away some funds from every paycheck. The longer you have accounts and the longer and more consistently you have been able to save money, the better you will look in the eyes of the lender when you are ready to apply for a mortgage loan in the future.

Can You Afford to Pay a Mortgage Each Month?

If you pay rent each month, you may be prepared to make monthly mortgage payments. The amount of your monthly payment depends on the amount you borrow, the interest rate on the note, and the repayment period or term of the loan. The shorter the term, the higher your monthly payment. For that reason, most home buyers repay their mortgage over the longest term possible, usually 30 years. If you know how much you need to borrow (the sales price less your down payment) and what the interest rate will be, you can use Table 11.1 to find out what your monthly payments will be with a standard 30-year, fixed-rate mortgage. The table includes principal and interest payments only and does not reflect collection for property taxes or insurance.

While the costs vary depending on where you live and the cost of your home, they can add a hundred dollars or more to your monthly payment. If you are thinking about buying a unit in a condominium project or cooperative building, or a house in a planned unit development (PUD), you also may need to pay monthly homeowner's fees to cover maintenance expenses or special assessments related to the common areas or even additional monies for projects on lease land.

TABLE 11.1
Loan Payments for a 30-Year, Fixed-Rate Mortgage

Loan Amount	Interest Rates						
	7%	7.5%	8%	8.5%	9%	9.5%	10%
$50K	$333	$350	$367	$384	$402	$420	$439
55K	366	385	404	423	443	462	483
60K	399	420	440	461	483	505	527
65K	432	454	477	500	523	547	570
70K	466	489	514	538	563	589	614
75K	499	524	550	577	603	631	658
80K	532	559	587	615	644	673	702
85K	566	594	624	654	684	715	746
90K	599	629	660	592	724	757	790
95K	632	664	697	730	764	799	834
100K	665	699	734	769	805	841	870

The interest rates shown in this table can help you calculate your monthly mortgage payment. For instance, if you bought a house for $80,000 with a down payment of $10,000 and you closed your 30-year loan at an interest rate of 8.5 percent, your monthly payment of principal and interest would be $538. This payment does not cover the property taxes or the hazard insurance that would be required, nor the mortgage insurance you may need to pay because your down payment is less than 20 percent.

How Much of a Loan Can I Qualify for in the Fannie Mae Program?

Lenders use two commonly accepted guidelines to determine your ability to make mortgage payments. These guidelines were briefly discussed earlier in this chapter, but Fannie Mae's requirements are a little different from those of the FHA or VA.

Your lender will look closely at your individual financial situation to determine if more flexible guidelines are appropriate for you. If your real estate agent does not have a formula for figuring out what you can qualify for, he or she should have access to a mortgage banker or lender who can provide this service before you begin looking at homes: Know what you can qualify for.

Your monthly housing costs including mortgage payments, property taxes, homeowner and mortgage insurance, and homeowner's fees should total no more than 20 percent of your monthly gross income (gross income is income before taxes are taken out). In addition to your regular pay, your income can include funds received from overtime, bonuses, a part-time job, a second job, retirement, VA and Social Security benefits, disability, welfare and unemployment benefits, alimony and child support, your monthly housing costs plus other long-term debts such as car payment (over 10 months to pay), student loans, or other installment debts; these should total no more than 36 percent of your monthly gross income.

Depending on your household income, you may be eligible for special assistance programs. These programs may make it easier for you to get a larger mortgage loan than you normally would be able to obtain using the qualifying rules. To get an idea of the mortgage amount that you might be able to qualify for based on your annual income, review Table 11.2. This table does not include taxes and insurance, which would add approximately 3% to the amount shown. If you know the approximate current interest rate and the annual income shared by your family, Table 11.2 should give you an idea of what loan amount you should be able to qualify for. Check the real estate section of your local newspaper or call a mortgage company or bank to get the current interest rates for your area.

The table uses only the qualifying ratio for housing expense (25% housing expense); It assumes you have no other existing debt. If you have car payments or other bills due monthly, the amount you can borrow would be decreased. This takes care of the *first qualifying rule, your housing expense ratio*.

The following examples of home mortgage qualifying should give you an idea of how you can or cannot fit into Fannie Mae's qualifying criteria. Please also review the sample prequalifying worksheet (Exhibit 11.1).

TABLE 11.2

Mortgage Amounts Based on Annual Income

| Interest | Annual Income | | | | |
Rates (%)	$20K	$25K	$30K	$35K	$40K
7.0	$62,630	$78,290	$93,940	$109,600	$125,260
7.5	59,590	74,990	89,390	104,280	119,180
8.0	56,780	70,980	85,180	99,370	113,570
8.5	54,190	67,740	81,280	94,830	108,380
9.0	51,780	64,730	77,680	90,620	103,570
9.5	49,550	61,940	74,330	86,720	99,110
10.0	47,480	59,350	71,220	83,090	94,960
10.5	45,550	56,940	68,330	79,710	91,100
11.0	43,750	54,690	65,630	76,570	87,510

If you have previously tried to buy a home but were unable to get approved for a home loan, you should try to find out why the lender did not want to make the loan. Filling out the worksheet may help you determine on your own why you have been turned down in the past. You may have had an unstable work history, you may have attempted to purchase a home that was too expensive for your income, or your debt level was too high. If you cannot figure out why you have been turned down, contact your lender or banker for an explanation.

You can contact Fannie Mae at 1-800-832-2345 and request a list of lenders in your area who will be able to assist you in your effort to make the American dream of homeownership come true.

Example 1. The borrower has an allowable housing expense of $665 and a house payment of $541. He then meets the qualifying ratio for housing expense because he is under the 28% qualifying bracket. He is actually at 22% housing expense. In the total debt ratio, he is allowed to have $855 worth of debt with his new housing expense. He fits under the 36% allowable (34.1%) and therefore qualifies incomewise.

Single borrower's gross annual salary	$28,500
Divide by 12 months	÷12
Total monthly income	$ 2,375
Monthly gross income	$ 2,375
Multiply by 28% (allowable housing expense)	×.28
Allowable monthly housing costs	$ 665
Home purchase price	$60,000
Down payment	−5,000
Mortgage loan amount	$55,000
30-year loan at 8% interest monthly payment (PI)	$ 404
Monthly taxes and insurance (estimate high end)	+137
Monthly mortgage payment	$ 541
Monthly gross income	$ 2,375
Multiply by 36% (allowable total debts w/housing)	×.36
Allowable total monthly debt	$ 855
Other monthly debts	
Car payment	$ 220
Credit cards	+50
Total other monthly debts	$ 270
Total monthly housing costs	$ 541
Total other monthly debts	+270
Total monthly costs	$ 811

Example 2. A married couple shows a housing expense to be 22% which is below the 28% guideline, but because of the existing revolving debt, plus the new house payment, their total monthly costs put them at a 47% ratio, which is above the 36% allowable by Fannie Mae guidelines. Therefore these buyers would not qualify for a loan.

Gross annual salary (husband and wife combined)	$30,000
Divide by 12 months	÷12
Total monthly income	$ 2,500
Monthly gross income	$ 2,500
Multiply by 28% (allowable housing expense)	×.28
Allowable monthly housing costs	$ 700
Home purchase price	$59,000
Down payment	−4,000
Mortgage loan amount	$55,000
30-year loan at 8% interest monthly payment (PI)	$ 404
Monthly taxes and insurance (estimate high end)	+150
Monthly mortgage payment	$ 554
Monthly gross income	$ 2,500
Multiply by 36% (allowable total debts w/housing)	×.36
Allowable total monthly debt	$ 900
Other Monthly Debts	
Car payment	$ 200
Student loan	110
Credit cards	+320
Total other monthly debts	$ 630
Total monthly housing costs	$ 554
Total other monthly debts	+630
Total monthly costs	$ 1,184

12 UNDERSTANDING THE LOAN APPLICATION AND FORMS

When applying for a home loan, the following information should help you understand the process and enable you to expedite your transaction with the lender in a timely fashion.

The loan application, commonly referred to as a "Form 1003" by the lender, is where the process begins. This is assuming you have previously been qualified by your lender either by phone or in person prior to making an offer on the home you wish to purchase. The more complete the application and information brought in by you, the buyer, the easier it is for the lender to compile your paperwork and eventually render a decision of approval.

The loan application is an important step toward homeownership. For most transactions, whether they are FHA, VA, or conventional financing, you'll need to bring the following with you:

1. Copies of your driver's license and Social Security cards.

2. Most recent bank statements or copy of your passbook, or certificates of deposit of all accounts listed on the application.

3. If self-employed, accruing commissioned or bonus income, your most recent two years' tax returns (1040s),

a year-to-date profit and loss statement, a balance sheet, and business license.

4. If your income is based on interest, dividends, or rental income, you will need to submit 1040s again, along with copies of rental agreements or any promissory notes that show the amount owed and the interest being received.

5. If your income includes Social Security or pension income, award letters and copies of most recent checks received for these payments. (If the payments are automatically deposited into your accounts, three months' bank statements will be needed. *Note:* Highlighting the deposit helps prove this income.)

6. If involved in any partnerships, copies of your K-1's (partnership returns or 1065s) and if you are incorporated, corporate tax returns or 1120s.

7. If not self-employed, W-2 forms for the past two years.

8. Most recent paycheck stubs from all borrowers to be involved in the transaction.

9. Name and address for your landlord for the past two years (this is for verification of creditworthiness in making your rental payments). This verification can be very helpful if you are a buyer with no credit or have had minimal usage of credit in the past.

10. If you are a veteran trying to obtain a VA loan, your DD-214 (the copy of your discharge).

Assuming you are cooperative and have brought in or supplied the requested information, it would be time to begin filling out your loan application. Believe it or not, it would be in your best interest to have the lender ask the questions and complete the application for you. Too many applications are returned because they are incomplete.

THE FORM 1003 HOME LOAN APPLICATION

Section I: Type of Mortgage and Loan Term

The mortgage you are applying for should be checked in the appropriate boxes listed: VA, FHA, conventional, FmHa (Farmers Home Loan) or *other* (this could be a private party or hard money, but should be identified).

The *Agency Case Number* should be completed by the lender. If you are applying for an FHA Loan, a case number would be issued by the Federal Housing Administration; if you are applying for a VA loan, a LHG number (loan home guarantee) would be placed in the agency case number box. The last box (lender case number) is for the lender's loan number. Although many lenders refer to their files by the borrower's last name, all loans are issued a loan number.

Section II: Property Information and Purpose of Loan

This section basically asks whether you are purchasing or refinancing the home, or whether it is a construction loan that would have to be refinanced for permanent financing, or for any other purpose (e.g., second trust deed or home improvement). The next boxes you will check or not check in Section II are whether or not this property will be your primary residence, secondary residence (second home or vacation home), or investment property (rental property). The reason for this is that the difference in money down changes dramatically when buying a home as your primary residence (anywhere from 0% to 5% down); a second home can be 20 percent down, and an investment property 25 percent down.

The next box refers to title and how it will be held, (e.g., John D. Smith and Mary R. Smith, as husband and wife in joint tenancy). Some lenders would suggest you check with an attorney on how to hold title, depending on your own situation. "Joint tenancy" basically is the right of survivorship. If John D.

Smith was to die, Mary R. Smith would have to get a copy of his death certificate, and an affidavit of death, have it recorded with the title company in the county in which the property is recorded. And title would go into her name, usually like this: Mary R. Smith, a Widow. People who buy homes with their friends or a significant other have the option of claiming title as "tenants in common." With this provision, they can "will their interest." For example, Bruce D. Jones, a Single Man, and Michael S. Smith, a Single Man, can take title as tenants in common or can have the option of survivorship, depending on their own personal situation.

The next box to check is whether or not the property is fee simple, or a leasehold estate. Fee simple means you own the land, where as a leasehold means you are living in the property to buy, but you are paying the owner of the land a monthly lease payment (this should be disclosed to you in your purchase contract). In southern California and throughout parts of the United States, you will come across both privately held lease land and Indian owned lease land. The lender usually requires that the lease term be at least 15 years longer than the mortgage term, so if you purchase a home or condominium in 1996, and your loan term is 30 years or due in the year 2026, the lease term on the land should be over the year 2041.

The last box in Section II asks for your source of down payment and settlement charges and/or subordinate financing. Most borrowers use resources via their verifiable savings and checking accounts, but resources can also be obtained through gift, liquidation of a pension, money against a retirement plan, or through the refinance of another property. Be careful because you can list the money for down payment and closing costs as borrowed, as long as these funds can be traced and the new payment is figured into your qualifying ratios.

Section III: Borrower Information

This section starts out with borrower and coborrower. If you are applying for a loan and are using a coborrower or cosigner, you must *each* fill out Form 1003, with the exception of those who are cohabiting and have savings, checking, and credit held jointly. Always fill out your name completely, first, middle, and last. Your Social Security numbers, home phone numbers, and age are all self-explanatory. Years in school would be 12 (through high school), plus any years of college.

The next boxes have to do with marital status. If you are married, so indicate; if you are unmarried but were previously married, the lender will request further information to prove whether or not you are responsible for child support, alimony (if you receive child support, this would be additional income to help you qualify). Usually if a woman checks single on an application and has been previously married, her maiden name or married name will appear under an "also known as" or "aka" on her credit report. This is a red flag for the lender, so always be on the level with your loan officer.

The next question is the present address section. Your lender needs to know where you have been living for the past two years, so they can rate how you pay your rent; if not paid on time, or if you show moving from place to place, you are likely to appear somewhat unstable.

Section IV: Employment Information

This section deals with name and address of your employer, how long you have been on the job, how long you have been in the same line of work or profession, what your position is, and the business phone number. If your spouse is not working, the term "home maker" or "student" may be appropriate. If you have held your present position less than two years, then you have to supply information for previous employers. In qualifying for a home loan, you must show that you are, or have been, in the same line of work for at least two years or that you have been earning a degree or learning a trade related to what you are currently doing, if less than two years. Remember, when you are applying for a home loan, you have just entered an information highway in which cross-checking employment, addresses, and credit is just the beginning.

Section V: Income Information and Housing Expense

Section V begins with the question, What is your income? Go down the seven boxes on the left side. The first asks for base monthly income. If you are on a salary, you would put your base in this box. If you are paid by the hour, your lender can take your hourly pay, multiply it by 40 hours, then multiply that by 52 (weeks in the year) and divide by 12 to obtain your monthly base. The second and third boxes are for overtime and bonuses. Overtime and bonuses are only figured into additional income if they have been given on a regular basis for the past two years, or can be verified by the employer that they will continue. The fourth box is for commissions. Commissions are figured in for people who are in commission-only positions or receive a base, plus commission. On your Form 1040s, if you are receiving commission income, lenders will look for a 2106 (business-related expenses form) to obtain accurate qualifying information. Dividends and interest income, the fifth box, can be verified by the tax returns and interest statements prepared by your stock and/or bond broker. Net rental income, the sixth box, is looked at by obtaining your income tax return and looking at Schedule E, which will show rent losses, expenses, depreciation, and so forth.

You would show other income, the seventh box, if you, the borrower, had two jobs. You can use the income from a second job only if you have been on the second job for at least two years, or if you were going to school during that time to obtain the second job while still employed on your first job.

After obtaining your totals for monthly income, the lender (assuming you took my advice and are filling out the application with him or her) will ask you about your current housing expenses. If you are paying rent, it is self-explanatory. If you have a mortgage payment, it should be broken down into principal, interest, taxes, and insurance, plus any homeowner association dues, land lease payments, and so forth. The far column is your proposed expenses, or what you will be paying. The reason for this is to prove that you will not have what lenders call "payment shock." A lender does not want you to have a house payment of $1,000 per month if you have been renting for $400 per month unless your income changes to warrant the new lifestyle. You can also use alimony and/or child support as other income.

Section VI: Assets and Liabilities

This section covers your assets and liabilities, the left side being your assets and the right side being your liabilities. The overall end result between your assets and liabilities is called "net worth."

In the first box under Section VI (page two of Form 1003), "Cash deposit toward the purchase held by:" you would name the escrow company, real estate company, or attorney holding the check that you presented as deposit in good faith when you wrote the offer on the house, indicating the amount of the deposit. The next four boxes are for your bank accounts. You should have with you the names, addresses, account numbers, and balance information at the time you complete the loan application.

The next question has to do with stock and bond information. You should have an idea as to the worth of your stock and the number of shares, so a value can be placed on this asset. After that, list life insurance with a cash value. The face value of insurance is the amount your beneficiary would receive on your death; the cash value of the policy is the amount available to you in the form of a savings plan. At this time, you would subtotal your liquid assets (assets that can be immediately turned to cash). The next asset box is for real estate owned. If you currently own any real estate, it should be listed on page 3 of Form 1003 under Section VI.

Vested interest or retirement fund information refers to an individual retirement account (IRA), or a 401(k) pension plan through your employment. Automobiles should be listed with make and models; "other assets" include all personal property you own—jewelry, tools, clothing, personal belongings, boats, jet skis, or anything else that you could put a value on if it were lost or stolen. Look through your home one day and think about what it would cost to completely replace your valuables. It can run up into many thousands of dollars; most people usually fill this box in with anywhere from $50,000 to $100,000.

The liabilities section of the loan application should be filled out as completely and as accurately as possible. There are seven boxes for you to list your credit cards, the names of the credit card companies, the approximate balance, and the payment. A lender will take down 5 percent of the balance as your payment, unless a credit card statement is provided. If you provide all your credit card statements, this will help your qualifying ratios. You must also list any student loans, furniture store loans, jewelry loans, or any lines of credit you are paying on other than just credit cards. If you have any car payments, you must list these also. And finally, child support, alimony and any job-related expenses must be listed before computing your "net worth."

The last part of Section VI is for the borrower who already owns real estate. You are to include the property address (including city, state, and zip code), type of property (sold, pending sale in escrow, or rental). Then you should have an idea what the property is worth, or the fair market or present value. How much is owed on this property (the balance of your note)? What is the gross rental income you are receiving—the rent money you are collecting before making the payment? What is the actual mortgage payment, interest included, plus the insurance, maintenance, and taxes? This should leave you with your last box, which would give the lender the information on the amount of net rental income.

Section VII: Details of the Purchase

This section covers the details of the purchase and is usually filled out by the lender or the lender's loan processor. Under the small letter "A" in this section would be the purchase price of the property in question, and down the line whether it is a refinance or purchase. Box "P" would give you the cash amount needed to close the loan and escrow or, if it is a refinance, the cash to be given to the borrower or owner. A good faith estimate should be prepared by the lender prior to the filling out of a loan application so you go in knowing approximately how much money will be needed and what your payment will be.

Section VIII: Declarations

These are "yes" and "no" answers to 13 questions about you and your coborrower:

A. Are there any outstanding judgments against you? If you had an outstanding judgment, I can guarantee you would know about it. A judgment is usually awarded when you are sued by someone for lack of payment or loss. A satisfied judgment would be listed on your credit report and if a judgment was paid but not satisfied, a copy of the canceled check and a satisfaction of judgment should be recorded through the court that awarded the judgment. A good lender should know how to rectify this situation.

B. Have you been declared bankrupt within the past 7 years? (Again, a "yes" or "no" question.) Remember that bankruptcy does not necessarily mean "no loan." There are requirements listed in this book based on how old the bankruptcy is and your credit situation after the fact. These are always going to be the deciding factors on loan approval, provided job stability, income, and cash reserves are all in order.

C. Question "C" relates to foreclosure and/or deed in lieu of foreclosure in the past seven years. If this is the case, notify your lender because if you are applying for government-insured loans, you could be eligible. You should obtain a "caver" number from HUD (credit alert hot line). This will tell you whether you are eligible for FHA financing or VA financing once again. This can only be obtained by the "HUD-approved lender" you are dealing with.

D. Question "D" asks if you are party to a lawsuit. The reason for this is that if you obtain ownership and lose a lawsuit, the property can be attached and therefore will be open to the possibility of a clouded title.

E. This question regarding contractual obligations to any government agency or body includes but is not limited to student loans, small business administration, and previous FHA or VA loans that might have resulted in foreclosure. They ask that you give in detail, a letter of explanation and loan numbers for any loan in this category. Sometimes a loan could have gone into foreclosure if someone assumed a loan that previously was in your name. A release of liability form should have been recorded in such a case. Please keep in mind this does not necessarily mean that you are ineligible for new real estate financing.

F. This question has to do with obligations that are currently being paid, for which you're in a delinquent position. If you were to give details as to why your obligations are currently late, such as temporarily being on disability, death of a wage earner, or another reason that might be out of your control, consideration will still be given.

G. Are you obligated to pay child support, alimony, or separate maintenance? This is asked on page 2 of the

Form 1003 in Section VI, so be careful to be consistent in your answers.

H. Is any part of the down payment borrowed? Be careful here, because this is asked in Section I, on page 1 of Form 1003, under source of down payment and settlement charges. You may borrow money against another property you own, to buy the one you are applying for, providing you disclose the new debt.

I. Are you a comaker or endorser on a note? This question seeks to find out whether you are obligated elsewhere, not previously disclosed in the body of the application. This information can affect qualifying ratios, if you are. If you have cosigned for another home and you want to buy one now, you have to prove that the coborrower has made a minimum of the past 12 payments by providing canceled checks or copies of cashier's checks purchased by the other borrower to prove *you* have not been making the payments.

J. Are you a U.S. citizen? There are two reasons for asking this question: to monitor who is receiving home loans in the United States and is to find out whether you are a citizen or a resident alien.

K. Are you a permanent resident alien? Permanent resident aliens can buy real estate in the United States.

L. Do you intend to occupy the property? This is a basic "Yes" or "No," but it will affect your down payment. On FHA loans, I have witnessed people buy with little down; they check this box "yes" and never move in themselves. I have also witnessed those loans being called due for "uninsuring" reasons. If FHA will not insure the loan, the lender stands to lose up to 25 percent of the sales price in the event of a default.

M. The final question has to do with whether or not you have had property interest in the past three years and in what way you carried title. This is basic, but can make a difference in determining whether or not you are actually going to occupy the property.

Section IX: Acknowledgment and Agreement

This section states that you are in agreement with the information provided on the loan application. To the best of your knowledge, all information is true and correct under penalties of perjury and possible fines or imprisonment. Always read the fine print carefully on *anything* you sign.

Section X is for government monitoring purposes, and the information asked of you is voluntary. They want to know if you are American Indian, Alaskan Native, Black, Hispanic, Asian, White, Male or Female. You cannot be discriminated against when completing this section of the application.

ESSENTIAL FORMS

The following are the titles of forms you will have to sign with your loan application and explanations thereof.

Housing Financial Discrimination Act of 1977 Fair Lending Notice

It is illegal to discriminate in the provision of or in the availability of financial assistance because of the consideration of trends, characteristics, or geographic changes surrounding a neighborhood or a housing accommodation, unless the financial institution can demonstrate in that particular case that such consideration is required to avoid an unsafe and unsound business practice.

It is also illegal to discriminate against race, color, religion, sex, marital status, national origin, or ancestry. If you have questions as to the preceding factors, or you feel you have been discriminated against, your lender should provide the address of the Department of Savings and Loan, and/or the State Department of Real Estate for the state in which you are buying.

Equal Credit Opportunity Act
Fair Lending Notice

The Federal Equal Credit Opportunity Act prohibits creditors from discriminating against credit applicants on the basis of race, color, religion, national origin, marital status, age (provided that the applicant has the capacity to enter into a binding contract), because all or part of the applicant's income derives from a public assistance program, or because the applicant has, in good faith, exercised any rights under the Consumer Credit Protection Act.

Fee Collection Form

Each lender is different, but the majority of mortgage bankers will have a form disclosing how much money is collected at the time of the loan application (fees usually collected for appraisal and credit). On the same form might be a "cancellation fee" agreement; this could call for a $100 charge if the loan has not been submitted and approved. If the loan is approved, the lender could ask for 1 percent of the loan amount in addition to a nonrefund for monies on appraisal and credit.

Important Notice to Applicant (Form)

This disclosure states that the interest rates and discount fees will fluctuate until the time of loan approval. Most lenders will offer you, the buyer, an option to "lock" at time of application. The problem is that if you take a "lock" on your rate and the rates go down, you are stuck with the higher interest rate. Interest rates quoted to you at time of your loan application or any time during the loan process are quoted as current market information only. Your loan may close at a higher or lower interest rate and fee, dependent on the trend of the market at the time your loan is approved.

On this form is a disclosure of interest rates and fees. As defined under interest rates and fees, the interest rate and fee can be guaranteed only after obtaining loan approval. Once your loan has been "locked" for a guaranteed period, your interest rate and fees will be protected against upward interest rate fluctuations.

If your loan does not close within the guaranteed period, your loan will be repriced at either the original guaranteed rate and fees, or the then current price, whichever is higher. Once your loan is "locked," your interest rate and fees can never be lower than the original price (as quoted by the lender you're working with). This form should disclose the interest rate as of the date of your signing the loan application and whether it is a fixed rate or variable rate, along with the discount points being charged.

Borrower's Blanket Signature Authorization Form

This form is an authorization for the lender to check into your bank account information, employment verification, credit reporting agencies, and any other information deemed necessary to obtain loan approval. On this form should be a notice that is required by the Right to Financial Privacy Act of 1978 that HUD/FHA has a right of access to financial institutions in connection with the consideration or administration of assistance to you. Financial records involving your transaction will be available to HUD/FHA without further notice or authorization but will not be disclosed or released by this institution to another government agency or department without your consent (except as required or permitted by law). In lay terms, your records regarding employment, credit, and so forth, are now available to the Department of Housing and Urban Development and/or the Federal Housing Administration for auditing, monitoring, or investigating purposes.

Assumption of HUD/FHA Insured Mortgages
Release of Personal Liability Form

Read this carefully. You are legally obligated to make the monthly payments required by your mortgage (deed of trust) and promissory note. The Department of Housing and Urban Development (HUD) has acted to keep investors and noncreditworthy purchasers from acquiring one to four family residential properties covered by certain FHA-insured mortgages. There are minor exceptions to the restriction on investors: loans to public agencies and some nonprofit organizations; loans under special mortgage insurance programs for property sold by HUD; rehabilitation loans or refinancing of insured mortgages. Your lender can advise you if you are included in one of these exceptions.

HUD will therefore direct the lender to accelerate this FHA-insured mortgage loan if all or part of the property is sold or transferred to a purchaser or recipient (1) who will not occupy the property as his or her primary or principal residence or secondary residence, or (2) who does occupy the property but whose credit has not been approved in accordance with HUD requirements. (This policy will apply except for certain sales or transfers where acceleration is prohibited by law.)

When a loan is accelerated, the entire balance is declared "immediately due and payable." Since HUD will not approve the sale of the property covered by this mortgage to an investor or to a person whose credit has not been approved, you, the original homeowner, would remain liable for the mortgage debt even though the title to the property might have been transferred to the new buyer.

Even if you sell your home by letting an approved purchaser (a creditworthy owner/occupant) assume your home mortgage, you are still liable for the mortgage debt unless you obtain a "release of liability" from your lender. FHA-approved lenders have been instructed by HUD to prepare such a release when an original homeowner sells his or her property to a creditworthy purchaser who executes an agreement to assume and pay the mortgage debt and thereby agrees to become the "substitute mortgagor." The release is contained in Form HUD 92201-1 (Approval of Purchaser and Release of Seller). You should ask for it if the mortgage lender does not provide it to you automatically when you sell your home to a creditworthy owner/occupant purchaser who executes an agreement to assume personal liability for the debt. When this form is executed, you are no longer liable for the mortgage debt.

Homeowners Fact Sheet Form Regarding Mortgage Insurance Premium Refunds and Distributive Shares (Form) for FHA-Insured Loans

When a mortgage premium is paid in a one-time payment at the time of mortgage closing, the borrower will be eligible for a refund of any unearned premium if the insurance is terminated prior to the maturity of the mortgage with no insurance claim involved. HUD began the one-time premium system in September 1983, for a limited number of insurance programs. If you are not sure that the mortgage insurance premium (MIP) was paid in full at loan closing, ask your lender. You do not need to be the original borrower to be eligible for a refund.

If you buy a home, wherein you refinance and pay off an existing FHA loan, you could be eligible for the previous owner's refund of unused mortgage insurance premium because you assumed the original note, which included this premium. Refunds of mortgage insurance premiums are based on the original loan amount, the years remaining on the mortgage, and the interest rate of the note. You can contact the lender for an actual refund amount after the sale of your home, or if you refinanced the former FHA loan for an applicable MIP refund. When termination of FHA insurance is required before maturity of a mortgage, the lender submits a Form HUD-2344 to HUD, which is a lender's request for termination of home mortgage insurance. For maturities the lender responds to HUD's request for confirmation that the mortgage is paid in full. In either instance, the lender provides HUD with the current address of the borrower. HUD determines whether a refund of MIP is due. If so, HUD sends a claim to the borrower for signature and returns it to HUD. This form is normally sent within 90 days after termination.

After receipt of the signed form, HUD has the payment mailed to the borrower. Payment is normally made within 45 days after receipt of the claim form. For those qualifying for payment, it is important to provide a forwarding address to the lender at the time of mortgage insurance termination so that HUD can send the claim form to the proper location. The borrower should verify that the lender furnished a current mailing address to HUD.

Regarding Assumptions.   When an FHA-insured mortgage is assumed, the insurance continues in force and there will be no refund. Unearned mortgage insurance premiums in this case where the original borrower financed the one-time MIP will not be refunded, the assumptors assume the payments of the remaining MIP as part of the total mortgage payment. On the other hand, when the original borrowers paid the one-time MIP in cash, they would not be able to recover from HUD that portion which might be considered unearned premiums unless they negotiate with the assumptors in a side agreement. HUD will not become involved in these negotiations.

Requests for information regarding mortgage insurance and mortgage insurance premium refunds should be sent to:

U.S. Department of Housing and Urban Development
Director, Mortgage Insurance Accounting and Servicing
Attn: Insurance Operations Division
Washington, DC 20410

Another form required for signature is an FHA form titled "Warning: Watch out for Lead Paint Poisoning" and is applicable to homes constructed prior to 1978.

Watch out for lead paint poisoning if you buy an old home. A child can get lead poisoning by eating bits of paint that contain lead. A child who eats enough lead paint may suffer brain damage, become mentally retarded, or in some cases, die. Older houses often have layers of lead paint on the walls, ceilings, and in the woodwork. When the paint chips off or when the plaster breaks, there is real danger for infants and young children. Outdoors, lead paints and primers may have been used in many places, such as walls, fences, porches, and fire escapes. If you see your child putting pieces of paint or plaster in his or her mouth, take the child to a doctor immediately. In the beginning stages of lead poisoning, a child may not appear really ill; do not wait for signs of poisoning.

There are additional forms you might need to sign or be familiar with.

Forms Related to VA Loans

Verification of VA Benefit—Related Indebtedness No. 26-8937. This form is to be signed by the veteran on Line 5 and sent to the Veterans Administration for completion. It will tell the lender whether the veteran has any outstanding debts such as VA student loans or any other form of VA loans that have not been repaid or satisfied.

Request for Determination of Eligibility and Available Loan Guaranty Entitlement No. 26-1880. This form is signed by the veteran on Line 19. It is sent to the Veterans Administration accompanied by the veteran's DD214 (discharge papers) and will determine the veteran's amount of entitlement for a home loan.

Federal Collection Policy Notice. This form notifies the veteran the following procedures that will be taken in the attempt to collect on bad debts or late payments:

1. Your name and account information may be reported to a credit bureau.

2. Additional interest and penalty charges may be assessed for the period of time that payment is not made.

3. Charges to cover additional administration costs incurred by the government to service your account may be assessed.

4. Amounts owed to you under other federal programs may be offset.

5. Your account may be referred to a private collection agency.

6. Your account may be referred to the Department of Justice for litigation in the courts.

7. If you are a current or retired federal employee, your salary or civil service retirement benefits may be offset.

8. Your debt may be referred to the Internal Revenue Service for offset on any amount owed to you as an income tax refund.

9. Any written-off debt may be reported to the Internal Revenue Service as income.

All these actions can and will be used to recover any debts owed the Department of Veterans Affairs when it is determined to be in the best interest of the government to do so.

13 OBTAINING THE LOWEST INTEREST RATE

The lowest interest rates are always available to those borrowers who are a low credit risk, having what is referred to as "A" credit. Clearing up your credit can help you into the "A" borrower category, which will be explained in the next chapter.

There are many variables when shopping for a home loan, but usually the government-backed insured mortgages offer the lowest in fixed interest rates and the safest adjustable rates. Let me explain the adjustable-rate mortgage and how it works.

Because the adjustable-rate mortgage has a lower start rate, it is easier for a buyer with high ratios to qualify for a loan. The adjustable-rate mortgage is tied into an "index" of certificates of deposit that fluctuates according to what the bank is paying for its money or what the bank is paying its depositors for their money.

The adjustable-rate mortgage, which usually starts out up to 3 percent lower than the fixed rate, is called a "teaser" rate and is intended to attract borrowers. Depending on the national index the rate is tied to, it can go up usually 2 percent annually, or 1 percent every six months.

When considering an adjustable-rate mortgage, ask your lender what the "margin" is on the loan. The margin is basically the bank's profit on the loan. Your cost of funds, plus your margin will put you at your interest rate, after your teaser rate runs out.

The next thing to consider is the "life cap." This is the ceiling on the loan (the highest it can go). If your start rate is at 6 percent, your life cap is 6 percent, and your annual cap is 2 percent, then a worst case scenario at the end of three years, would give you an interest rate of 12 percent. Depending on the amount of money borrowed, this could represent a drastic increase in your current monthly payment. Remember, you're qualifying on the "teaser" rate, not the rate that the loan could reach if inflation were to hit the interest rate market.

Another thing to consider when applying for an adjustable-rate mortgage is whether or not the loan you are applying for has a "conversion" option. This would allow you to convert the adjustable rate to a fixed rate during the loan period. This is a relatively new program, and most lenders offer the conversion option to their borrowers structured in such a way that after the 24th month and up to the 60th month (from beginning of the third year to the end of the fifth year), you would be able to change to a fixed rate. Most people consider this option too late in the process because in a downward interest rate market, such as the refinance era from 1986 through 1994, conversion options often have expired; likewise, by the time a borrower sees that interest rates are on the rise, it is too late to convert, (not worth the time or money to do so).

The advantage of an adjustable-rate mortgage is that you qualify on the lower start rate, which could put you in a larger house with a bigger sales price than would be possible if you were to purchase at a fixed rate. If you're planning on buying and only staying short term (less than three years), you could save the money between your lower start rate and the current fixed rate for the first year, or up to three.

The disadvantage of an adjustable rate loan is that you have no control of the index it's tied to, and you'll always be unsure what your payment will be. I have had hundreds of clients refinance their adjustable-rate loans to fixed rates when the rates were coming down, all because of the uncertainty of the loan they previously had.

Depending on the adjustable term and index, some banks offer a three-year fixed-rate loan that becomes adjustable after the first 36 months. If you plan on buying a house to fix it up for resale, the adjustable-rate loan might be the program for you.

Be careful if you consider an adjustable-rate mortgage with a balloon payment. This means that at the end of a certain time frame, usually five to seven years, if the house is not sold or refinanced, the loan becomes due and payable in full.

Your lender should be able to direct you to the best loan program available. Don't be afraid to ask questions; after all buying real estate is the biggest financial decision most people ever make. Find out if the loan you are obtaining is assumable and whether or not there is a prepayment penalty.

This is a good question because some loans have prepayment penalties. A lender can have provision in the deed of trust calling for up to six months worth of interest if the loan is paid off within the first three to five years, depending on how the contract reads. Or you could be charged a flat fee called "points" which equates to a percentage of the loan balance. For example, you owe $150,000 and you decide to refinance the loan. If the loan you are refinancing allows a prepayment penalty of 2 points for a payoff during the first 36 months, you would be charged 2 percent, or a $3,000 penalty. This could get expensive; banks prefer to sell this type of loan so be careful when choosing your loan program, especially if it is an adjustable-rate mortgage. Another way to get a lower interest rate when purchasing real estate is to buy down the rate with "discount points."

Most loan programs charge points. On a conventional loan, the points are the charge by the mortgage company or bank for doing the loan. But, in a government-backed loan such as FHA or VA, the points charged are to obtain a certain interest rate. If you purchase a home in a tract, sometimes the builder or developer will pay up to three discount points for their borrowers. This can reduce the interest rate by up to .75 percent and save you $40 to $100 per month depending on the loan amount and sales price of the home.

When working with real estate agents, it is good to make the offer with the seller paying the buyer's discount points, so you can obtain the lowest interest rate available. The seller may say "no" or make a counteroffer for only one or two points; but if you don't ask, you will never know whether or not you could have bought the rate down.

In your quest to make the American dream of home ownership come true, be careful when undertaking any real estate transaction and always consult an attorney or real estate broker before entering any contract. Examine any documentation that has to be signed or notorized and make sure you know what you're signing.

14 CREATING FINANCE— CLEANING UP THE MESS

I will explain what you need to know about credit and how you can personally clean up your own, thus becoming creditworthy again. The philosophy behind cleaning up the mess is understanding that sometimes circumstances beyond a person's control can affect the average American; a failing economy frequently sparks such circumstances such as factory closings and shutdowns of military bases or installations. Thousands of small businesses fail because of economic crises, many of which are related to natural disasters such as earthquakes (California), hurricanes (Florida), tornados (the Midwest), floods (Oklahoma, California).

Other "circumstances beyond our control" include unexpected medical problems, the death of a wage earner, and so on. These personal situations put a majority of people into a "credit risk" position, evidenced by a series of late payments showing on their credit report. Creditors cannot afford to be concerned about your particular "sad story"; they have an obligation to report those late payments and collection problems.

It pays to have a good payment history or credit record. Individuals who have fallen on hard times causing late payments or credit problems, pay a high price; they are constantly charged higher interest rates, pay more in finance charges, and undoubtedly would be required to pay a much larger down payment for any purchase.

When you get a speeding ticket, it comes off your driving record after three years, but a late payment or collection can plague your credit report for as long as seven years. And that is how a bank or financial institution sees late-paying customers—they are a true credit risk. I know it seems like kicking a person who is down, but that's where my cleanup techniques come into play.

First of all, I don't consider people with slow, poor, or even bad credit, as losers. You shouldn't either. We all deserve an opportunity to create finance and clean up our credit mess. That is not to say that there won't always be a certain percentage of "deadbeats" that think the world owes them something, but according to collection agencies that percentage is as low as 2 percent.

HOW TO DISPUTE YOUR DEROGATORY CREDIT BY PHONE BEFORE TAKING MEASURES IN WRITING

Rule No. 1, is a rule to live by when clearing credit: *Prove it or remove it!* Believe it or not, major corporations have a way of losing information. In fact, large department stores keep client information on their computer system for as little as 24 months, sometimes only 12 months. This is to your advantage! If you dispute a late payment that has been reported to TRW, Trans Union, or Equifax (the three largest credit-reporting agencies), that late payment will stay on your credit for up to seven years. If your creditor cannot provide you with statement of "account activity," by law, that creditor must send a deletion letter to the agency or agencies that received the report.

Please keep a conversation log of any calls to creditors, listing the name of the individuals you've spoken with along with their phone numbers and extensions. If you call a creditor on an account showing a late payment that was due to an address change, they will usually cooperate with you, especially if you are in current "good standing" with them. When contacting a major corporation (e.g., Bullocks or J.C. Penney), you could be talking to a credit representative in a room with as many as one hundred people running computers. Remember, everyone's personality is different. One day, Mrs. Smith might respond negatively with, "No, we won't remove that," and the next day Mr. Jones might say, "Yes, we will delete the derogatory mark" (you should receive a copy of the letter sent to the credit reporting agency for your records).

Are you familiar with the term, "a Friday or Monday car"? When you're having car problems, the mechanic may tell you the car probably came off the assembly line on Friday (when people can't wait for the weekend to begin), or Monday (when no one is real excited to be back at work). This can apply when speaking to creditors in an attempt to clear credit. Some days are better than others. That is why I won't stop at one phone call when clearing a client's credit. I will continue to call until I get the answer I need and I will do so by going right up the ladder to supervisors, department heads, or whomever. When I'm doing a home loan for a client, I have only 30 days or so to clean up a credit report. This is a service for which I receive no additional compensation, (it is illegal to receive compensation undisclosed to a real estate broker outside normal commissions). I do this for my clients because I want to see them have the American dream come true by being able to buy a home. And if you're attempting to clear your credit on your own, be cautious of your time frame. You can easily go beyond 30 days, so you should set a firm goal for completion if you're interested in making the changes necessary to qualify for that "low down," better interest rate finance.

If you're ready to take on the creditors, the first step is to order a full factual credit report; this can be handled through your bank or mortgage company. It will cost approximately $50 and will include reports from TRW, Trans Union, Equifax, and Public Record. Once you've received a copy of your report, sit down and analyze your credit situation. Each account you've had in the past will be listed. Reading from left to right, the columns will show the name of the creditor, account number, last date reported, the date the account was opened, the highest credit, the payment terms, the balance owing, the amount past due, account type (such as revolving, installment, real estate, or other), and furthest to the right, your 30-, 60-, or 90-day lates.

In regard to any late payments showing, my suggestion is to respond by phone first. Most companies provide 1-800-numbers which will not only save you money, but phone calls are less time consuming than mailing letters. Dispute in writing only if you have no success with your phone calls. Let me state some facts that will help you.

If a company is no longer in business and its name appears on your credit report showing a late payment, or several, the credit-reporting agency will automatically remove the information when it is disputed in writing (information that is unverifiable, or not available). When a company is no longer in business, the reported information on the credit report becomes inaccurate and must be removed. Remember, *"Prove or remove."*

With the savings and loan scandal, hundreds of banks have been taken over by the Resolution Trust Corporation (RTC). If you've ever called them, you will have discovered that you receive one answer from one person and something else from another.

The bottom line is that often the only information they have would be considered "basic," and they usually cannot respond to a dispute, much less comply within the 30 days allowed by law (as reasonable time) to provide information or remove derogatory status. Again, *"Prove or remove."*

A number of department stores have either merged (e.g., Robinson's and May Company) or have filed a Chapter 11 bankruptcy, a business move for the reorganization of large corporations. If a merger occurs, the credit department transfers all *existing accounts* from one to another. If your account is "inactive" but previously showed as "late" or "slow pay," they usually will purge this information and list it only as a "paid off" or "closed account"; it becomes too time-consuming to provide previous credit information and becomes more cost-effective to list the card as a "closed account" (no liability). Once again, the information previously reported becomes inaccurate because no record or documentation is available ("prove or remove").

I have dealt with thousands of customer service representatives and find they're very cooperative, especially if they're "regrouping," as they *are* interested in your business. In the event of a company takeover or buyout, the existing credit will usually be assumed (e.g., collections, late payments). The same rules apply for assigned accounts, unless you have an existing account. Your previous pay information is most likely unavailable and is listed as "closed account 0 balance." The *only* information available is what was originally reported to credit repositories (TRW, Trans Union, Equifax).

COLLECTIONS AND COLLECTION AGENCIES

The services of a collection agency can be used by anyone and are not limited, as you might think, to department stores, banks, car dealers, and credit holders. Doctors, hospitals, utility companies, and private parties use collection agencies.

Collection agencies are governed by the Fair Debt Collection Practices Act (FDCPA) and must follow the guidelines (Regulation Z) set by Federal Credit Reporting Laws. Collection agencies often walk a fine line where harassment is concerned. They may contact you at work unless they are advised you are not allowed to take this type of call while on the job. I had a client getting phone calls at 9:30 P.M. at her place of employment, a violation of both the Fair Debt Collection Practice Act, and of the Equal Credit Opportunity Act (ECOA) because it was not a reasonable hour, and the agency had been advised not to call at work. I told my client to file a formal complaint with the Federal Trade Commission and the Better Business Bureau. The collector was fined and warned that in the future, these violations could affect the current license of the company.

Working for a collection agency as a customer service representative is much more difficult than holding the same type of position for a department store. This is not a friendly business; consider dealing all day with people who have unkept promises to pay. There's also the problem of tracking people down, the threats to sue or attach wages, and other unpleasant tasks.

You will find a good number of collections occur when insurance companies "underpay" a medical bill. Most hospitals use outside agencies to collect deficiency balances; this is how this type of collection can end up on your report. A collection company usually has the documentation provided by the agency or hospital to whom the money is owed. Once this collection is paid, the collection agency lists it as a "paid collection" and will not delete it.

The best way to handle this is to contact the original creditor; although they are no longer collecting on the bill, they have the authority to direct or request a deletion letter to be sent both to you and the credit-reporting agencies.

If a collection agency is local, take the time to go in person; you will find them a little more cooperative. They have the authority to remove some collections without checking with the original creditor. Keep in mind, as a rule of thumb, if the bill was paid within 30 days of notification, they will usually delete.

I have, at times, gone over the head of the customer service department, directly to the owner, to inquire whether or not they have a deletion fee policy. A deletion fee is a charge by the collection agency to delete the credit notation. If they do, this could save you the time of disputing for removal in writing. This should be used only as a last resort because when you dispute in writing, the credit notation will eventually be removed.

After speaking first to the collection agency, it is best to go to the original creditor and advise them payment was made in full and you expect the credit notation to be deleted because the original creditor can authorize deletions; they will usually cooperate when your credit report shows an "open collection." There is no way to dispute an open collection on your record until it's been negotiated, but you are in a bargaining position. I suggest to my clients that they begin negotiating at 50 percent of the existing balance (not counting any accrued interest). Although you owe this money collection agencies are willing to cooperate because they work for a percentage. When you make a settlement offer, request the collection be deleted from credit agencies. You will be told they will show the collection as "paid"; then you can negotiate higher for a deletion.

For example, I had a client who owed a bank approximately $1,200 on a credit card that had been assigned to a collection agency, I was informed that, with interest, my client owed over $1,600. Authorized by my client, I made an offer to the collector: If he would delete the account from all credit-reporting agencies, my client would have $1,000 in the form of a cashier's check, federal expressed (good funds) on his desk the following morning, no later than at 10:30 A.M. "Yes," was the answer, and the credit collection was deleted. Keep in mind, this money was owed; however, it was settled for less and still deleted. If I had not gotten the deletion by phone, my client would still have had to pay off the account before disputing in writing. My client saved $600 in unpaid principal and accruing interest, and probably another $200 in charges for employing an agency to clear his credit line. You can save hundreds or even thousands depending on your case history.

Please remember to ask for your deletion letter or agreement to delete in writing, for your personal records, before payoff.

REPOSSESSION

Disputing or negotiating a repossessed vehicle can be tough. Follow the basic steps. If the original creditor is no longer in business, information might not be available. Dispute this in writing. In most cases, the original amount is that amount that will show as "owing" when a bank or financial institution, credit union, or whoever finances this loan takes a vehicle back. They either sell it, give it to a dealer on consignment or auction it off. The balance on the loan, plus any legal fees, less the price obtained on the resale of the vehicle, is the deficiency balance. If they can prove this, then you go to your negotiating position (before disputing in writing).

I have settled deficiency balances for clients for as low as 45 percent. Because banks usually put such accounts in a "charge-off" position and write them off on their profit and loss statement, they are usually willing to negotiate. This payoff is handled by a department usually labeled "recovery." Do not forget to remind them that you are requiring a deletion letter on settlement. If they will only change status to "paid repossession," follow the steps to dispute in writing for removal.

My results of credit worthiness once again are guaranteed if you follow the basic steps, rules, and regulations. Keep a conversation log of those individuals you have contacted and set up a file for your certified mailing, which is explained in Chapter 15.

Example 1: Mr. and Mrs. Bruzzels. My clients, Mr. and Mrs. Bruzzels, needed help to obtain financing. I pulled up a full factual credit report for the Bruzzels, and it showed the following information: There was one 90-day-late payment with Broadway; three 30, two 60, and four 90-day-late payments with Rocky Mountain Bancard Visa. Sears showed five 30-day late payments; Western Savings and Loan showed two 30-day-lates. This covered the late payments. There was additional derogatory credit such as a Ward's charge-off with an unknown amount owing, a GMAC repossession with an unpaid balance of $4,391, A Valley Creditor Collection, United Acceptance "unpaid collection" $437, Buffums "paid collection," Broadway Southwest "paid collection," and finally, Coachella Valley Collections Services, unpaid collection with a balance of $456.

What lenders in their right mind would tell their clients, "Yes, I can get you a low-money-down FHA loan"? With credit like this? There was some work to do here and with the authorization and cooperation of my clients, I was able to do the entire "clearing" by phone. I did not have to write a single dispute letter. I called the credit-reporting agency and got the phone numbers for all creditors showing any derogatory credit. By calling each account individually, I found that a majority of the delinquencies were no longer on the creditor's computer system. I helped negotiate a settlement with GMAC for $1,900, and discovered that the Coachella Valley Collection was an unpaid veterinarian debt (the dog had died and there was reason for not paying the collection). The credit report then met the criteria set forth by the Federal Housing Administration and the Veterans Administration. Sears was dropped to one 30-day-late; GMAC and the veterinarian's bill on Bruzzels' credit report were dropped to paid collections but could still be removed by disputing it in writing, if they chose to continue with the process. However, I felt we were in a position to present a letter of explanation on the three accounts instead.

Here's how we fared before and after starting the loan process.

Before		After	
30-day-lates	10	30-day-late	1 (Sears)
60-day-lates	2	60-day-late	0
90-day-lates	4	90-day-late	0
unpaid coll.	4	unpaid coll.	0
paid coll.	3	paid coll.	2

The Bruzzels would have paid a $500 deposit to a credit fix agency and an additional $2,000 for this many lines of derogatory credit, with no guarantees nor specified time frame. In the Bruzzels case, their credit was cleaned up during a normal escrow period.

Example 2: Mr. Murray. Mr. Murray was applying for an FHA loan and stood no chance (with five collections), of qualifying for the financing. Three of the collections were unpaid. Once again, I wrote no letters (made no disputes in writing) but negotiated a deletion on all five accounts (see following chapters for negotiation procedures). I knew I would have to get all five collections deleted or the deal would not fly. I did it in less than one week. The finished product, or cleared credit report that followed indicated that there were "no trades developed," meaning no established credit. Remember, "No credit is better than bad credit." Once the collections were removed and showed Mr. Murray had no established credit, I supplied a current rental rating, showing he paid his rent on time, as well as an accumulation of paid utility bills for the past six months to prove creditworthiness. The loan was approved.

15 CLEANING UP CREDIT IN WRITING

I was in a restaurant in Rancho Mirage, California, one night, celebrating a friend's birthday. When the waiter approached our table, I recognized him as one of my previous clients—Harry was someone who had been continually turned down on financing a home. His credit record had been a serious problem. He looked at my friend and said, "If it wasn't for this man, my family and I would not be living in the home that we have now. Nobody but him would help us. Thought we'd be renting forever." His grateful words were followed by a complimentary bottle of wine, and as he poured us each a glass, he said, "This one's on me." Well, Harry, I won't forget, and it's that pleasure of helping someone attain the American dream that has inspired this book.

In this chapter, I will explain the credit-clearing process and how to dispute lines of credit appearing on your credit report so you can bring back a good credit rating and fulfill your own dream of homeownership.

In this age of computer wizardry, all consumers should monitor their credit standing. The "big three" credit-reporting agencies often give misleading and incorrect information about consumers; it happens every day. According to the National Consumer Research Organization, 7 out of every 10 credit profiles contain incorrect information that can damage a person's character and credibility.

If you understand the value of restoring credit, receiving additional credit cards, and establishing new credit, you understand what it will afford you. Restored credit allows you to buy a home with a better interest rate, finance cars, pay off debts that originated at a higher interest rate, refinance 19 percent credit lines to 8 percent, and establish some form of savings.

COLLECTION AGENCIES

The Federal Fair Debt Collection Practice Act, along with state regulations (e.g., in California, the California Robbins-Rosenthal Fair Debt Collection Practices Act) and other statutes, are just some of the many regulatory commissions that affect collection practices. The Bureau of Collection and Investigative Services is part of the Department of Consumer Affairs, which comprises 38 separate regulatory agencies. The Chief of the Bureau is directly responsible to the Director of the Department. The Director has a broad range of powers and responsibilities in the protection of California consumers as mandated by the Consumer Affairs Act of 1970.* The bureau regulates the practices and businesses for collection of debts owed to other individuals or businesses. Regulation of the collection agency industry includes licensure of the agency, certification of the agency's manager, and registration of all but clerical and sales employees. In regulating the collection agency industry, the Bureau strives to protect the consumer/debtor from false, deceptive, and abusive practices, and to protect businesses that refer accounts for collection from financial loss.

Enforcement and Discipline

Collection agency owners and employees must abide by the statutes and regulations governing the collection of debts and

---

*Although the majority of my business is in California, the laws are similar from state to state.

an agency's relationship with its customers. Licensees, certificate holders, and registrants are responsible for knowing the laws and rules that govern their conduct and the possible consequences of unlawful practices.

The enforcement of debt collection laws and regulations is a primary function of the Bureau. The Bureau's efforts focus on achieving voluntary compliance by licensees, deterring and disciplining violators, and removing from the industry those individuals who have been determined unfit to engage in collection activity. Depending on the number and severity of violations by a licensee, certificate holder, or registrant, the Bureau may take the following actions:

1. Issue a notice of warning.

2. Conduct an office conference with the Bureau Chief, or designee, discussing the activity of an agency, or individual, manager, or agency owner.

3. Conduct an audit or a formal investigation.

4. Appoint a conservator to an agency when trust account violations occur; the conservator assumes control of the agency and its assets and recommends the most appropriate disposition of the agency to the Director.

5. Prepare an accusation against appropriate licenses. The Bureau is represented by the Attorney General's Office, and the matter is heard by an administrative law judge who proposes a decision to the Director. The Director may adopt, amend, or reject the proposed decision, which may recommend suspension or revocation of the licenses. The Director's decision can be challenged in court by the licensee.

6. Violations that may constitute criminal conduct will be referred to the Division of Investigation, and may thereafter be submitted to the appropriate prosecuting authority for possible criminal prosecution.

Federal Fair Debt Collection Practices Act

This act applies to the collection of consumer debts and not commercial (business) debt. Here are the findings and purposes of this act:

> There is abundant evidence of the use of abusive, deceptive, and unfair debt collection practices by many debt collectors. Abusive debt collection practices contribute to the number of personal bankruptcies, marital instability, loss of jobs, and individual privacy.
>
> Existing laws and procedures for redressing these injuries are inadequate to protect the consumers. Means other than misrepresentation or other abusive debt collection practices are available for effective collection of debts. Abusive debt collection practices are carried on to a substantial extent in interstate commerce and through means and instrumentalities of such commerce. Even where abusive debt collection practices are purely intrastate in character, they nevertheless directly affect interstate commerce.
>
> It is the purpose of the Federal Fair Debt Collection Practices Act, Title VIII, to eliminate abusive debt collection practices by debt collectors, and to insure that those debt collectors who refrain from using abusive debt collection practices are not competitively disadvantaged, and to promote consistent state action to protect consumers against debt collection abuses.

The following definitions for words used in the Federal Fair Debt Collection Practices Act will be recognized throughout its contents:

> *Commission*   Federal Trade Commission.
>
> *Communication*   The conveying of information regarding a debt directly or indirectly to any person through any medium.
>
> *Consumer*   Any natural person obligated or allegedly obligated to pay any debt.

Creditor   Any person who offers or extends credit creating a debt or to whom a debt is owed. But such term does not include any person to the extent that he/she receives an assignment or transfer of a debt default solely for the purpose of facilitating collection of such debt for another.

Debt   Any obligation or alleged obligation of a consumer to pay money arising out of a transaction in which money, property, insurance, or services, being the subject of the transaction, are primarily for personal, family, or household purposes, whether or not such obligation has been reduced to judgment.

Debt Collector   Any person who uses any instrumentality of interstate commerce or the mails in any business the principal purpose of which is the collection of any debts, or who regularly collects or attempts to collect, directly or indirectly, debts owed or due asserted to be owed or due to another.

State   Any state, territory, or possession of the United States, the District of Columbia, the Commonwealth of Puerto Rico, or any political subdivision of any of the foregoing.

Acquisition of Location Information (What Is Allowed by Law)

Any debt collector communicating with any person other than the consumer for the purpose of acquiring location information about the consumer shall do the following: (as found in the Federal Fair Debt Collection Practices Act)

1. Identify himself/herself, state that he/she is confirming or correcting location information concerning the consumer, and, only if expressly requested, identify his employer.
2. Not state that such consumer owes any debt.

3. Not communicate with any such person more than once unless requested to do so by such person or unless the debt collector reasonably believes that the earlier response of such person is erroneous or incomplete and that such person now has correct or complete location information.

4. Not communicate by postcard.

5. Not use any language or symbol on any envelope or in the contents of any communication effected by the mails or telegram that indicates that the debt collector is in the debt collection business or that the communication relates to the collection of a debt.

6. After the debt collector knows the consumer is represented by an attorney with regard to the subject debt and has knowledge of, or can readily ascertain, such attorney's name and address, not communicate with any person other than that attorney, unless the attorney fails to respond to communication from the debt collector within a reasonable period of time.

The next section on communication in connection with debt collection has some restrictions, some of which often get collection agencies in trouble for noncompliance.

Federal Fair Debt Collection Practices Act: Section 805

Without the prior consent of the consumer given directly to the debt collector or the express permission of a court of competent jurisdiction, a debt collector may not communicate with a consumer in connection with the collection of any debt.

1. At any unusual time or place or time or place known or which should be known to be inconvenient to the consumer. In absence of knowledge of circumstances to the

contrary, a debt collector shall assume that the convenient time for communicating with a consumer is after 8:00 o'clock ante meridian and before 9:00 o'clock post meridian, local time at the consumer's location.

2. If the debt collector knows the consumer is represented by an attorney with respect to such debt and has knowledge of, or can readily ascertain, such attorney's name and address, unless the attorney fails to respond to a communication from the debt collector within a reasonable period of time or unless the attorney consents to direct communication with the consumer.

3. At the consumer's place of employment if the debt collector knows or has reason to know that the consumer's employer prohibits the consumer from receiving such communication.

Communication with Third Parties

Without prior consent of the consumer given directly to the debt collector, or the express permission of a court of competent jurisdiction, or as reasonably necessary to effectuate a postjudgment judicial remedy, a debt collector may not communicate in connection with the collection of any debt, with any person other than the consumer, his attorney, a consumer reporting agency, if otherwise permitted by law, the creditor, the attorney of the creditor, or the attorney of the debt collector.

Ceasing Communication

If a consumer notifies a debt collector in writing that the consumer refuses to pay a debt or that the consumer wishes the debt collector to cease further communication with the consumer, the debt collector shall not communicate further with the consumer with respect to such debt, except:

1. To advise the consumer that the debt collector's further efforts are being terminated.

2. To notify the consumer that the debt collector or creditor may invoke specified remedies which are ordinarily invoked by such debt collector or creditor.

3. Where applicable, to notify the consumer that the debt collector or creditor intends to invoke a specified remedy. If such notice to the consumer is made by mail, notification shall be complete upon receipt.

Harassment or Abuse

A debt collector may not engage in any conduct the natural consequence of which is to harass, oppress, or abuse any person in connection with the collection of a debt, without limiting the general application of the foregoing, the following conduct is a violation of section *806.00 of the FFDCPA:*

1. The use or threat of use of violence or other criminal means to harm the physical person, reputation, or property of any person.

2. The use of obscene or profane language or language the natural consequence of which is to abuse the hearer or reader.

3. The publication of a list of consumers who allegedly refuse to pay debts, except to a consumer-reporting agency or to persons meeting the requirements of this act.

4. The advertisement for sale of any debt to coerce payment of this debt.

5. Causing a telephone to ring or engaging any person in telephone conversation repeatedly or continuously with intent to annoy, abuse, or harass any person at the called number.

6. The placement of telephone calls without meaningful disclosure of the identity of the caller (except) as in Section "Acquisition of Location Information."

False or Misleading Representation

A debt collector may not use any false, deceptive, or misleading representation or means in connection with the collection of any debt without limiting the general application of the foregoing. The following conduct is a violation of this section:

1. The false representation or implication that the debt collector is vouched for, bonded by, or affiliated with the United States or any state, including the use of a badge, uniform, or facsimile thereof.

2. The false representation of the character, amount, or legal status of any debt, the false representation of any services rendered for compensation which may be lawfully received by any debt collector for the collection of a debt.

3. The false representation or implication that any individual is an attorney or that any communication is from an attorney.

4. The representation or implication that nonpayment of any debt will result in the arrest or imprisonment of any person or the seizure, garnishment, attachment, or sale of any property or wages of any person unless such action is lawful and the debt collector or creditor intends to take such action.

5. The threat to take any action that cannot legally be taken or that is not intended to be taken.

6. The false representation or implication that a sale referral, or other transfer of any interest in a debt shall cause the consumer to lose any claim or defense to payment of the debt, or become subject to any practice prohibited in this title (FFDCPA).

7. The false representation or implication that the consumer committed any crime or other conduct in order to disgrace the consumer.

8. Communicating or threatening to communicate to any person, credit information which is known or which should be known to be false, including the failure to communicate that a disputed debt is disputed.

9. The use or distribution of any written communication which simulates or is falsely represented to be a document authorized, issued, or approved by any court, official, or agency of the United States or any state, or which creates a false impression as its source, authorization, or approval.

10. The use of any false representation or deceptive means to collect or attempt to collect any debt or to obtain information concerning a consumer.

11. Except as otherwise provided for communications to acquire location information, the failure to disclose clearly in all communications made to collect a debt or to obtain information about a consumer, that the debt collector is attempting to collect a debt and that any information obtained will be used for that purpose.

12. The false representation or implication that accounts have been turned over to innocent purchasers for value.

13. The false representation or implication that documents are legal process.

14. The use of any business, company, or organization name other than the true name of the debt collector's business, company, or organization.

15. The false representation or implication that documents are not legal process forms or do not require action by the consumer.

16. The false representation or implication that a debt collector operates or is employed by a consumer reporting agency.

Unfair Practices as Determined by FFDCPA

A debt collector may not use unfair or unconscionable means to collect or attempt to collect any debt. Without limiting the general application of the foregoing, the following conduct is a violation:

1. The collection of any amount (including any interest, fee charge, or expense incidental to the principal obligation) unless such amount is expressly authorized by the agreement creating the debt or permitted by law.

2. The acceptance by a debt collector from any person of a check or other payment instrument postdated by more than five days unless such person is notified in writing of the debt collector's intent to deposit such check or instrument not more than 10 nor less than 3 business days prior to such deposit.

3. The solicitation by a debt collector of any postdated check or other postdated payment instrument for the purpose of threatening or instituting criminal prosecution.

4. Depositing or threatening to deposit any postdated check or other postdated payment instrument prior to the date on such check or instrument.

5. Causing charges to be made to any person for communications by concealment of the true purpose of the communication. Such charges include, but are not limited to, collect telephone calls and telegram fees.

6. Taking or threatening to take any nonjudicial action to effect dispossession or disablement of property if there is no present right to possession of any property claimed as collateral. Through an enforceable security interest, or there is no present limitation to take possession of the property, or the property is exempt by law from such dispossession or disablement.

7. Communicating with a consumer regarding a debt by postcard.

8. Using any language or symbol, other than the debt collector's address, on any envelope when communicating with a consumer by use of the mail or telegram, except that a debt collector may use his business name if such name does not indicate that he is in the debt collection business.

The information provided here is for your knowledge in the event you are currently in collection; you should know what rights you have as collection agencies and collectors make their attempts to obtain money owed. Understanding a debt collector's process can be useful to you in your attempt to obtain a clear credit standing.

The Fair Credit Reporting Act or (FCRA) is the guide (rules and regulations) for credit-reporting agencies. If you have ever applied for a charge account, a personal loan, insurance, or a job, someone is probably keeping a file on you. This file might contain information on how you pay your bills, or whether or not you have been sued, arrested, or have filed bankruptcy. The companies that gather this information are called "consumer-reporting agencies," or "CRAs." The credit bureau is the most common type of CRA. Credit bureaus sell information to creditors, employers, insurers, and other businesses in the form of "consumer reports." This generally contains information about where you work, live, and how you pay your bills (habits).

In 1970, Congress passed the Fair Credit Reporting Act (enforced by the Federal Trade Commission) to give consumers specific rights in dealing with CRAs. The Act protects you by requiring credit bureaus to furnish correct and complete information to businesses to use in evaluating your applications for credit, insurance, or a job. Please consult the back of the book for addresses to the Federal Trade Commission and other agencies.

COMMON QUESTIONS OFTEN ASKED

Q. *How do I locate the CRA that has my file?*

A. If your application was denied because of information supplied by a CRA, that agency's name and address must be supplied to you by the company you applied to. Otherwise, you can find the CRA that has your file by calling those listed in the yellow pages under "Credit" or "Credit Rating and Reporting." Since more than one CRA may have a file about you, call each one listed until you located all agencies maintaining a file on you (see Reference Guide to Credit-Reporting Agencies and Bureaus in the back of the book).

Q. *Do I have the right to know what the report says?*

A. Yes! If you request it, the CRA is required to tell you about every piece of information in the report, and in most cases, the sources of that information. Medical information is exempt from this rule; however, you may ask your physician to try to obtain it for you if necessary. A CRA is not required to give you a copy of the report, although more and more are doing so. You also have to be told the name of anyone who received a report on you in the past six-month period. If your inquiry concerns a job application, you can get the names of those who received a report during the past two years.

Q. *Is this information free?*

A. Yes, if your application was denied because of information furnished by the CRA, and if you request it within 30 days of receiving denial notice (see obtaining free credit report forms). If you don't meet these requirements, the CRA may charge a reasonable fee, usually not more than $8.

Q. *What can I do if the information is inaccurate or incomplete?*

A. Notify the CRA. They're required to reinvestigate the items in question. If the new investigation reveals an error, a corrected version will be sent, on your request, to anyone who received your report in the past six-month period (job applicants can have corrected reports sent to anyone who received a copy during the past two years).

Q. *What can I do if the CRA won't modify the report?*

A. The new investigation may not resolve your dispute with the CRA. If this happens, have the CRA include your version or summary of your version of the disputed information in your file and in future reports (see forms following this chapter).

Q. *What debts are covered?*

A. Personal, family, and household debts are covered under the act. This includes money owed for the purchase of a car, for medical care, or for charge accounts.

I will explain the Fair Credit Reporting Act Sections that you will be referencing in the following sample letters and formats to be sent to the credit reporting agencies. These sections will explain the law and will be helpful in your attempts to clear your credit.

FAIR CREDIT REPORTING ACT

Section 602 Findings and Purpose

(a) The Congress makes the following findings;

    (1) The banking system is dependent upon the fair and accurate credit reporting. Inaccurate credit reports directly impair the efficiency of the banking system, and unfair credit reporting methods undermine the public confidence which is essential to the continued functioning of the banking system.

    (2) An elaborate mechanism has been developed for investigating and evaluating the creditworthiness,

credit standing, credit capacity, character, and general reputation of consumers.

(3) Consumer reporting agencies have assumed a vital role in assembling and evaluating consumer credit and other information on consumers.

(4) There is a need to insure that consumer reporting agencies exercise their grave responsibilities with fairness, impartiality, and a respect for the consumer's right to privacy.

(b) It is the purpose of this title to require that consumer reporting agencies adopt reasonable procedures for meeting the needs of commerce for consumer credit, personnel, insurance, and other information in a manner which is fair and equitable to the consumer, with regard to the confidentiality, accuracy, relevancy, and proper utilization of such information in accordance with the requirements of this title.

Section 611: Procedures in Case of Disputed Accuracy

(a) If the completeness or accuracy of any item of information contained in this file is disputed by a consumer, and such dispute is directly conveyed to the consumer reporting agency by the consumer, the consumer reporting agency shall within a reasonable period of time reinvestigate and record the current status of that information unless it has reasonable grounds to believe that the dispute by the consumer is frivolous or irrelevant. If after such reinvestigation, such information is found to be inaccurate or can no longer be verified, the consumer reporting agency shall promptly delete such information. The presence of contradictory information in the consumer's file does not in and of itself constitute reasonable grounds for believing the dispute is frivolous or irrelevant.

The section just quoted from the Fair Credit Reporting Act states that a reasonable period of time should occur for the consumer credit-reporting agency's investigation. When you send in your dispute letters, a clause should state that an assumption will be made that 30 days is a reasonable time for investigation. If they will not agree to that, then they should put in writing the time frame they will need. Understanding that credit-reporting agencies are forced to act quickly by the laws of the Fair Credit Reporting Act, will be helpful in your attempts to straighten up your credit profile.

Section 612: Charges for Certain Disclosures

A consumer reporting agency shall make all disclosures pursuant to Section 609 and furnish all consumer reports pursuant to Section 611(d) without charge to the consumer if within 30 days after receipt by such consumer of a notification pursuant to Section 615 or notification from a debt collection agency affiliated with such consumer reporting agency stating that the consumer's credit rating may be or has been adversely affected the consumer makes a request under 609 or 611(d). Otherwise a consumer reporting agency may impose a reasonable charge on the consumer for making disclosure to such consumer pursuant to Section 609, the charge for which shall be indicated to the consumer prior to making disclosure; and for furnishing notifications, statements, summaries or codifications to persons designated by the consumer pursuant to Section 611(d), the charge for which shall be indicated to the consumer prior to furnishing such information and shall not exceed the charge that the consumer reporting agency would impose on each designated recipient for a consumer report except that no charge may be made for notifying such persons of the deletion of information which is found to be inaccurate or which can no longer be verified.

By understanding the terminology of this section, you will be able to obtain free copies of your credit reports in your attempt to clean up any derogatory credit from your files.

FORM LETTERS
AND PROCEDURES

Your first step in cleaning up your credit or making credit changes is to obtain your credit report. If you have been denied credit, a request to the CRA that denied the credit, upon request, will give you a copy of your report. Because most creditors report to all three agencies, it would be a good idea to contact all three. Example 1 is a sample format.

EXAMPLE 1: REQUEST FOR CREDIT REPORT

TO: Trans Union Credit Information Service
       1561 E. Orangethorpe Avenue
       Fullerton, California 92634
       Attention Customer Service Relations Department:

I am formally requesting that you send me a copy of my credit report. All of the information you should need is listed below. I am also enclosing a check in the amount of $8.00 to cover the necessary expenses involved.

Name _____

Address _____

City/State/Zip _____

Social Security No. _____

Date of Birth _____

Signature _____

Note: The same form should be sent to TRW and Equifax:

TRW Credit Information Service
12606 Greenville Avenue
P.O. Box 749029
Dallas, Texas 75374
214-235-1200

CBI **Equifax** Credit Service
130 South State College
  Boulevard #100
Brea, California 92621
714-255-5641

EXAMPLE 2: REQUEST FOR FREE CREDIT REPORT

(After you have applied for and been denied a line of credit)

To: (CRA) TRW, Trans Union or Equifax (with their addresses)

From: Your name

According to the attached letter, sent by (fill in company), indicating my credit application has been denied, (name of credit agency) issued the report which was used for my credit decision. The Fair Credit Reporting Act of 1970, Section 609, provides the credit bureau should send me information which led to denying my credit application and according to the provisions of Section 612, there should be no charge for this information.

Please send my credit report to me at the address below. Additional information identifying my account is on the attached letter that denies me my credit.

Thank you very much.

Name _____

Address _____

City/State/Zip _____

Social Security No. _____

Date of Birth _____

Signature _____

Keep in mind that these forms are acceptable as shown, but other forms will need to be reproduced and handwritten because you do not want the CRA to think there is a third-party involvement; you don't want to run the risk of the CRA not cooperating with your request.

Once you have received your credit report(s), the next step is to send a complaint letter to delete inquiries.

EXAMPLE 3: SAMPLE COMPLAINT LETTER TO DELETE INQUIRIES

I have received a copy of my credit report and have found some errors (see the attached copy, with these items highlighted).

By the provisions of Section 611 of the Fair Credit Reporting Act of 1970, I demand these inquiries be reinvestigated and deleted from my credit file. I would like a list of parties (names and addresses) of anyone contacted on my behalf so that I can do my own follow-up work.

I shall assume that 30 days constitutes a reasonable amount of time for reverification of these entries, unless notified otherwise. I will expect that these items will be removed from my credit file if there is a failure to respond or reverify these items within the next 30 days; this would be considered a reasonable time frame according to the FCRA, Section 611A.

Also, pursuant to Section 611D, of the Fair Credit Reporting Act, please send me notification that the items have been deleted. You may send an updated copy of my credit report to the following address. According to Section 612 of the FCRA, there should be no charge.

Sincerely,

Signature _____

Name (Printed) _____

Address _____

City/State/Zip _____

Social Security No. _____

Date of Birth _____

EXAMPLE 4: MERGER OF INQUIRY TO NEW ACCOUNT

I have recently received my credit report from your company and have noticed the following inaccuracies; I am highlighting the problems that I have noticed, numbering same on the report itself.

The presence of inquiries as new entries separate from the result of a new account being opened, results in the inaccuracy on duplication of information. The inquiry reflects information to be incorrect, an inaccurate processing of my credit profile. (An inquiry becomes a new account but still shows as an inquiry.)

Under the provisions of the Fair Credit Reporting Act, Section 611A, please reinvestigate and delete these disputed inquiries. I would like a list of parties (names and addresses) of anyone contacted on my behalf so that I can do my own follow-up work.

I shall assume that 30 days constitutes a reasonable amount of time for reverification of these entries, unless otherwise notified. I will expect that these items will be removed from my credit file if there is a failure to respond or reverify these items within the next 30 days; this would be considered a reasonable time frame according to the FCRA, Section 611A.

Also, pursuant to Section 611D, of the Fair Credit Reporting Act, please send me notification that the items have been deleted. You may send an updated copy of my credit report to the following address. According to Section 612 of the FCRA, there should be no charge.

Sincerely,

Signature _____

Name (Printed) _____

Address _____

City/State/Zip _____

Social Security No. _____

Date of Birth _____

EXAMPLE 5: DELETION REQUEST FOR ACCOUNTS

I recently received a copy of my credit report and have found the following problems or inaccuracies. I am enclosing a copy of this report and have highlighted the areas in which I am disputing.

Under the provisions of the Fair Credit Reporting Act, Section 611A, please reinvestigate and delete these disputed inquiries. I would like a list of parties (names and addresses) of anyone contacted on my behalf so that I can do my own follow-up work.

I shall assume that 30 days constitutes a reasonable amount of time for reverification of these entries, unless otherwise notified. I will expect that these items will be removed from my credit file if there is a failure to respond or reverify these items within the next 30 days; this would be considered a reasonable time frame according to the FCRA, Section 611A.

Also, pursuant to Section 611D, of the Fair Credit Reporting Act, please send me notification that the items have been deleted. You may send an updated copy of my credit report to the following address. According to Section 612 of the FCRA, there should be no charge.

Sincerely,

Signature _____

Name (Printed) _____

Address _____

City/State/Zip _____

Social Security No. _____

Date of Birth _____

The following form is used when the credit report does not show an account as current as you know it is. Be sure to specify that this writing is in reference to: Request to Update Account.

EXAMPLE 6: REGARDING REQUEST TO UPDATE ACCOUNT

I recently received a copy of my credit report and have found the following problems or inaccuracies. I am enclosing a copy of this report and have highlighted the areas in which I am requesting an "update."

Under the provisions of the Fair Credit Reporting Act, Section 611A, please reinvestigate and "update" these disputed inquiries. I would like a list of parties (names and addresses) of anyone contacted on my behalf so that I can do my own follow-up work.

I shall assume that 30 days constitutes a reasonable amount of time for reverification of these entries, unless otherwise notified. I will expect that these items will be "updated" on my credit file if there is a failure to respond or reverify these items within the next 30 days; this would be considered a reasonable time frame according to the FCRA, Section 611A.

Also, pursuant to Section 611D, of the Fair Credit Reporting Act, please send me notification that the items have been "updated." You may send an updated copy of my credit report to the following address. According to Section 612 of the FCRA, there should be no charge.

Sincerely,

Signature _____

Name (Printed) _____

Address _____

City/State/Zip _____

Social Security No. _____

Date of Birth _____

EXAMPLE 7: REMINDER LETTER TO CRA TO RESPOND

Thirty days ago you received my letter disputing several items listed on my credit report by your firm; the items were highlighted for your convenience. I am including a copy of my letter to you.

Please realize that 30 days is considered a fair or reasonable amount of time under the Fair Credit Reporting Act, Section 611A for responding to my requests for verification of these items. Since you did not immediately write to inform me of the need for additional time, I presume the 30-day time limit was acceptable to you.

I have not received a reply from you within this 30-day time period. Therefore it must be that the information on my report is inaccurate, or it could not be reverified. In either event, according to the provisions of Section 611A the items must be deleted immediately.

Please respond immediately so that I do not need to pursue my legal rights under Sections 616 and 617 of the Fair Credit Reporting Act, which requires you to comply with the law.

Also, pursuant to Section 611D, of the Fair Credit Reporting Act, please send me notification that the items have been "updated." You may send an updated copy of my credit report to the following address. According to Section 612 of the FCRA, there should be no charge.

Sincerely,

Signature _____

Name (Printed) _____

Address _____

City/State/Zip _____

Social Security No. _____

Date of Birth _____

In some instances, the CRA will send out what they call a "reply to a frivolous letter." They will accuse you, the person trying to clean up your credit, as having third-party involvement, (this is when you hire a credit reporting agency or third party to handle your credit case). This is not illegal, but a deterrent on their part to have to do the additional work or investigation.

In this case your *handwritten* letter should state something to this effect:

EXAMPLE 8: RESPONSE TO A "FRIVOLOUS LETTER" REJECTION

Dear Sirs:

I recently received your letter stating that my request was "irrelevant and frivolous." I am very upset that your company would try such a blatant stall tactic. I am demanding that you reinvestigate my credit file and send an updated credit report within 30 days or delete the accounts in question.

Enclosed is another copy of my credit report with the disputed items highlighted. Any further stall tactics will be forwarded to the Federal Trade Commission.

Please send me names and addresses of everyone you have contacted on my behalf.

Sincerely,

Signature _____

Name (Printed) _____

Address _____

City/State/Zip _____

Social Security No. _____

Date of Birth _____

The following letter should be handwritten.

EXAMPLE 9: FINAL REQUEST TO CRA TO FOLLOW UP ON FAILURE TO RESPOND

On March 20, 1996 [make sure your date matches date you sent out your letter], I sent a letter to you to request a follow-up letter pointing out that you had failed to respond to my disputes of items highlighted and sent to you on my credit report, issued by your company. I have included copies of that letter and the dispute letter.

To this date, you have not fulfilled the intent and letter of the Fair Credit Reporting Act, which requires you, as a credit bureau, a consumer credit reporting agency, to maintain and insure that information "is fair and equitable to the consumer." Also, the law stipulates that bureaus will maintain "accuracy, relevancy, and proper utilization of such information" (Section 602, 4B). These requirements have not been met by your actions. You have not given me evidence that you have acted in a prompt, fair, and equitable manner.

1. You have not sent me the names and addresses of the people involved in the investigation, as requested, nor have I seen the removal of anything inaccurate.

2. You have not removed any item that could not be found within 30 days, (reasonable time).

3. You have not taken care to properly insure the information on my credit report is accurate, being proper information for my file.

I am still disputing the items given on my attached letter; I expect appropriate action to be taken on my behalf. If I don't receive the responses by _____ (date), I will contact the Federal Trade Commission to issue a complaint.

Sincerely,

Signature _____

Name (Printed) _____

Address _____

City/State/Zip _____

Social Security No. _____

Date of Birth _____

EXAMPLE 10: REQUEST FOR CORRECTED CREDIT REPORT

On _____ (date), I wrote to tell you I had not heard any specific actions taken to reverify the necessary items I had listed and highlighted on my credit report. These items are inaccurate (or incomplete) and I am attaching copies of my correspondence for your review.

Since you have not provided the names and addresses of the parties you contacted on my behalf for reverification of previous information, nor have you complied within the 30 days, accepted as reasonable time, I will assume that you have not been able to reverify the information I have disputed previously. Therefore, you must comply with the provisions of the Fair Credit Reporting Act, Section 611, and drop the disputed items from my credit history or profile.

I demand that you send me a copy of my updated credit report showing the elimination of the items which I disputed previously, and at no charge in accordance with Section 611D and 612 of the Fair Credit Report Act, respectively. I further demand that it be postmarked within five days after signing the certified mail receipt for the letter you are holding. If I do not receive an updated copy of my credit report, with the disputed items dropped, my attorney will pursue my legal rights under Section 616 of the Fair Credit Reporting Act, "Civil liability for willful noncompliance." Your credit bureau may be liable for the following:

1. Any actual damages I sustain by your failure to delete these items;

2. Punitive damages as the court may allow;

3. Costs of the court action, plus any attorney's fees. I have forwarded a copy of this letter to the Federal Trade Commission.

Sincerely,

Signature _____

Name (Printed) _____

Address _____

City/State/Zip _____

Social Security No. _____

Date of Birth _____

Use the following letter if you receive your credit report and notice a late payment.

EXAMPLE 11: DISPUTED DELINQUENT OR LATE PAYMENT (TO YOUR CREDITOR)

It has recently come to my attention that several (if applicable) of my payments to your company have been labeled "late" on my credit report. I felt I have been prompt in making my payments in the past, but might have been late due to the following reason(s):

[List reason(s): possible address change; forgot to sign the check; mailed out the wrong check to another creditor, etc.]

Since the late payments occurred for the reason(s) listed above, please correct the payment history for my account at the following credit bureaus which carry your account histories:

1. TRW (if applicable).
2. Trans Union (if applicable).
3. Equifax (if applicable).

It is important that my credit report reflect the good relations that I (or my spouse and I) have had with your company in the past and the correction on my credit report will make it more representative of my good financial habits.

I appreciate your assistance.

Sincerely,

Signature _____

Name (Printed) _____

Address _____

City/State/Zip _____

Social Security No. _____

Date of Birth _____

Account Number _____

This letter is used for adding good lines of credit to your credit profile.

EXAMPLE 12: REQUESTING ADDITION OF CREDIT HISTORY

Please include in my credit report the following information attached.

[Attach the names and account number of creditors that might not normally be reporting to the bureaus.]

According to the FCRA, Section 602B, "It is the purpose of this Act to require that consumer reporting agencies adopt reasonable procedures for meeting the needs of commerce for consumer credit, personnel, insurance, and other information in a manner which is fair and equitable to the consumer, with regard to the confidentiality, accuracy, relevancy, and proper utilization of such information in accordance with requirements of this Title." The intent of the FCRA includes recording supplementary credit information if requested by a consumer.

Accordingly, I hereby request that you add the attached history of payments to my credit profile.

Thank you for your cooperation. Please inform me within 30 days of your compliance with Section 611, requiring that a consumer's credit report should reflect completeness and accuracy, within a reasonable time after notification by the consumer.

Sincerely,

Signature _____

Name (Printed) _____

Address _____

City/State/Zip _____

Social Security No. _____

Date of Birth _____

GLOSSARY

Acceptance A legal term referring to the acceptance of an offer. A buyer offers to buy and the seller accepts the offer.

Acquisition cost The value of the property plus the FHA-allowed closing costs.

Adjustable-rate mortgage A mortgage loan that allows the interest rate to be charged at specific intervals over the term of the loan.

Agent One who is authorized to act for or represent another (principal) usually in business matters. Authority may be express or implied.

Amortization The liquidation of a financial obligation on an installment basis; also recovery over a period of cost or value.

Appraisal An estimate or opinion of value for a stated purpose as of a given date.

Assets All properties and claims against others that could cover liabilities.

Assumption of mortgage A method for guaranteeing a note. When a grantee takes title to real property and the deed contains an assumption agreement, or grantee executes a separate assumption agreement, the grantee becomes the principal guarantor for unpaid portions of the note and is primarily liable for the amount of any deficiency judgment.

Balloon payment   An installment payment on a promissory note—usually the final one for discharging the debt—which is significantly larger than the other installment payments in the terms of the promissory note.

Closing costs   The expenses and fees paid by the buyer and seller at the closing of a real estate purchase.

Cloud on title   Any condition revealed by a title search that affects the title to property. These are usually relatively unimportant items, but they cannot be removed without a deed or court action.

Commission   A payment for the performance of specific duties in real estate; a percentage of the selling price of property, percentage of rentals, and so forth.

Consideration   Anything of value given to induce entering into a contract; it may be money, personal services, or even love and affection.

Contract   An agreement, written or oral, to do or not to do certain things.

Debt-to-income ratio   The ratio between total monthly payments for debt and other fixed obligations (including proposed loan) and total monthly gross income.

Deed   A written instrument that, when properly executed and delivered, conveys title to real property.

Default   The failure to perform a required contractual duty. In terms of real estate financing, it refers to the failure of a borrower to continue to make regular payments on a mortgage loan.

Down payment   The difference between the purchase price of real estate and the mortgage loan amount.

Entitlement   In reference to a VA loan, the guarantee, or amount of the loan for which the VA becomes liable if the borrower defaults (25% of the maximum VA loan amount).

Equity   The interest or value which an owner has in real estate over and above the liens against it.

Encumbrance   Anything that affects or limits the fee simple title to property such as mortgages, trust deeds, easements, or restrictions of any kind, which do not prevent alienation of the fee title by the owner. Liens are special encumbrances that make the property security for the debt.

Escrow   The holding of monies and/or documents by a disinterested third party (the escrow agent) under specified terms and conditions, known as escrow instructions.

Federal Home Loan Mortgage Corporation (FHLMC; Freddie Mac)   A government agency with the designated purpose of serving as a secondary market facility for mortgages under the sponsorship of the Federal Home Loan Bank (the agency that supervises federal savings and loan associations).

Federal Housing Administration (FHA)   A federal agency that insures first mortgages, enabling lenders to loan a very high percentage of the sale price.

Federal National Mortgage Association (FNMA; Fannie Mae)   A private corporation dealing in the purchase of first mortgages, at discounts.

FHA loan   An institutional loan insured by the Federal Housing Administration. FHA loans are fully assumable.

Foreclosure   The legal process by which a lender's security interest in mortgaged real property is enforced (on default of the underlying loan) and the lien thereon satisfied. In its simplest form, the property is sold, the lienholder receives the proceeds to the extent of the lien, and the mortgagor receives any remaining funds (after expenses of sale).

Graduated payment mortgage (GPM)   A mortgage requiring lower payments in early years than in later years. Payments increase in steps each year until installments are sufficient to amortize the loan.

Homeowner's insurance Insurance that protects the owner from losses caused by most common disasters, theft, and liability.

Housing expenses Expenses that include mortgage principal and interest, homeowner's insurance, property taxes, mortgage insurance, homeowner's association dues, and ground rental charges.

Housing expenses-to-income ratio The ratio between total monthly payments from housing expenses and total gross monthly income.

Income property Property that produces income from residential or commercial rentals, and profits attributable to real estate other than rent.

Interest rate The percentage of a sum of money charged for its use.

Investment Money put in property or other ventures with the exception of making a profit, with sufficient security to return and protect the capital sum—not speculation.

Judgment A general lien; a final order of a court as the result of a lawsuit.

Lien A charge or encumbrance on property for the payment or discharge of an obligation.

Loan Grant of money or property for the use of another in exchange for the promise to repay the money or property, often including a charge for such use.

Loan origination The point at which a borrower secures a loan.

Mortgage An instrument by which property is hypothecated to secure the payment of a debt.

Mortgagee One who lends money under a mortgage.

Mortgage insurance premium (MIP) An insurance payment required by the FHA and paid for by the borrower to insure the lender against loss as a result of the borrower's default.

Mortgagor One who borrows money, pledging his or her property as security for repayment of the debt.

Negative Amortization An increase in the outstanding balance of a loan resulting from the failure of payments to cover required interest charged on the loan.

Negotiable Capable of being negotiated; assignable or transferable in the ordinary course of business.

Net worth The buyer's assets minus the buyer's liabilities.

Note A signed written instrument acknowledging a debt and promising payment.

Origination fee Amount paid by the borrower for the cost of issuing a loan.

Partnership A contract of two or more persons to unite their property, labor, or skill, or some of them, in prosecution of some joint and lawful business, and to share the profits in certain proportion.

PI Payment for principal and interest.

PITI Payment for principal, interest, taxes, and insurance, including homeowner's insurance.

Point Charges rendered by a bank for processing a loan; one point is one percent of the loan.

Prepayment clause Mortgage clause that allows the borrower to pay off the mortgage before it becomes due.

Prepayment penalty A sum payable in exchange for the right to repay a debt prior to the time it would otherwise be due.

Principal The amount of money owed on the mortgage and on which interest is paid.

Qualification The process of determining a buyer's eligibility for credit and/or ability to repay a credit obligation.

Qualifying The process of determining a buyer's eligibility for credit and/or ability to repay a credit obligation.

Refinancing   The process of getting a new loan to pay off an old one.

Satisfaction   The discharge of an obligation by paying a party what is due to that party (as on a mortgage, lien, judgment, or contract) or what is awarded by court.

Seller financing   The provision of financing to the buyer by the owner/seller of real estate who takes back a mortgage. The mortgage taken back can be a first mortgage (if no other outstanding financing exists on the property) or a second mortgage (if another loan secured by the property remains outstanding).

Subordinate   To make subject or junior to.

Tenancy-in-common   Ownership by two or more persons who hold undivided interests without right of survivorship.

Title   The rights of ownership.

Title insurance   Insurance written by a title company to protect the property owner against loss if title is imperfect.

Trust deed   An instrument that transfers (conveys) the bare legal title of a property to a trustee to be held pending fulfillment of an obligation, usually the repayment of a loan to a beneficiary.

VA loan   A fully assumable institutional loan, available to eligible veterans and guaranteed by the Veterans Administration.

Verification   Sworn statements before a duly qualified officer as to the correctness of the contents of an instrument.

Wraparound mortgage   (also called an all-inclusive trust deed, a hold harmless trust deed, an overriding trust deed or mortgage) The wraparound mortgage is a purchase money mortgage that is subordinate to, but yet includes the encumbrance or encumbrances to which it is subordinated.

Zoning   The division of a city or county by legislative regulations into areas (zones) specifying the uses allowable for the real property in these areas.

REFERENCE GUIDE TO CREDIT-REPORTING AGENCIES AND BUREAUS

American Association of Retired Persons (AARP)
601 E Street NW
Washington, DC 20049

Bureau of Collection and Investigative Services
1920 20th Street
Sacramento, California 95814-6873

CBI/Equifax Credit Services
130 South State College Boulevard No. 100
Brea, California 92621

Federal National Mortgage Association (Fannie Mae)
3900 Wisconsin Avenue NW
Washington, DC 20016-2899

Federal Trade Commission Headquarters
6th and Pennsylvania Avenue NW
Washington, DC 20580

Trans Union Credit Information Service
1561 East Orangethorpe Avenue
Fullerton, California 92634

TRW Credit Information Service
12606 Greenville Avenue
P.O. Box 749029
Dallas, Texas 75374

United States Department of Housing and Urban Development
Washington, DC 20410-8000

INDEX